"…the [illegible], or juvenile gigantomastia, in adolescence leads to a deforming and distressing condition during a sensitive period in a girl's life. Vulnerability to developing a negative body image and the desire to fit in predisposes these female adolescents to significant psychological stressors."

- PubMed

Simply Too Big

An 11-Year-Old Girl's Battle with

JUVENILE GIGANTOMASTIA

NICHOLA H WALKER

This edition first published in paperback by
Michael Terence Publishing in 2022
www.mtp.agency

ISBN 9781800944596

Michael Terence
Publishing

"Gigantomastia is a rare, psychologically and physically disabling condition characterised by excessive breast growth. To date, there is no universal classification or accepted definition for this condition."

JPRAS

To Our Daughter

"Tough times never last, but tough people do."

Robert H. Schuller

"Time and the hour runs through the roughest day."

William Shakespeare

"Above all, be the heroine of your life, not the victim."

Nora Ephron, Writer

"A really strong woman accepts the war she went through and is ennobled by her scars."

Carly Simon, Musical Artist

"You're going to walk into many rooms where you may be the only one who looks like you or who has had the experiences you've had. So you use that voice and be strong."

Kamala Harris, Vice President

Contents

Introduction 1
1: Motherhood and All That Jazz 3
2: How Big is Too Big? 10
3: BRAving the Storm 21
4: We're All Going on a Camping Holiday 29
5: The Very First Paediatric Consultation 35
6: First Cosmetic Surgery Consultation 42
7: You Cannot Be Serious! 49
8: Same Day and Second Cosmetic Consultation 59
9: The Great Reduction 65
10: The Weird and Wonderful! 76
11: Holidaying in the Land of the Free and the Home of the Brave 81
12: Here We Go Again… 87
12A: Hospital Photographs 96
13: A Double Dose of Sadness 98
13A: Photos On The Wild Side 109
14: Two Plus Two 111
15: How Much is that Doggy? 117
16: 'One Flew over the Cuckoo's Nest' 122
17: Backside Over Breast 126
18: The Old School Yard 132
19: The Intervening Years 137
20: Turkey or Bust 142
21: The Real Deal 148

22: Tit for Tat 153
23: Just When You Think It's All Over 158
24: Into the Future 166
25: Farewell 175
Lyrics 177
Acknowledgements 179
A Note from the Author 181

**"To be, or not to be – that is the question:
Whether 'tis nobler in the mind to suffer
The slings and arrows of outrageous fortune
Or to take arms against a sea of troubles.
And by opposing, end them?"**

William Shakespeare, Hamlet's Soliloquy

Introduction

In an honest, painful and at times, I hope, amusing memoir, I have charted the family's journey through the catastrophic illness of my daughter, Ellen, which not only destroyed her teenage years but the very prospect of life itself. I found myself expostulating and airing my grievances about issues that Ellen and our family were confronted with, and I might come across as seemingly heavy-handed and quick to blame, but at the time that was how I felt. My writing is not without its bias, and it must be understood and accepted within the context of the story. I expect and offer no excuses as no storyteller is completely objective.

During those years from 2006, when she was eleven years old, to 2014 when she was eighteen, I felt like I was in my own private war, fighting and protecting her from the slings and arrows of the world at large. Life had picked up every possible kind of ammunition and slung it at her. My daughter's body had turned against her by becoming an autonomous, operating vessel, never ceasing in its multiplication of breast tissue and severely sabotaging the life she once knew, causing the young girl that was my daughter to vanish when her cup size became the source of unwanted and all too frequent attention.

Outrageous fortune indeed.

The body is the instrument on which your life is played out; it must be kept well-tuned and in tip-top condition, anything less and the music becomes distorted, tuneless, and unpleasant to hear. Sadly, her body had become just that and the life she was able to lead was severely diminished, disrupted, and damaged.

To all those Mums with daughters, if you know something is not right, act upon it and believe in your intuition, in nearly all cases we do know better. Too big is 'Simply Too Big' and not, as we may well be told, on the outer edge of the growth spectrum. If there are other young girls who have had a similar medical history, I send you a big hug and to those who may be going through it, stand firm, believe in what you want and find out as much about your body as you can. At the end of the day, you only have one body and it's yours and yours alone.

In Ellen's own words:

I was so young and by default so fragile and it affected me in hugely negative ways, which still impact me now. There was no tool kit or guide to navigate my way through this period of my life, no one I knew was even remotely close to know or understand what I was going through, so I very much had to drudge it alone aged 11. Which in all honesty and looking back was lonely and damaging to a developing mind. The saying is true - misery loves company, and I'll admit I would have liked to have been less alone with my body which humiliated me on a daily basis. My coping mechanism was to remove myself from the present day and not really ever look in my reflection. All I could see was the top of my chest, bit like an iceberg I was unable to see the depth, which even though I knew was visible to all – it would offer temporary relief as I wasn't able to see the full scope of my chest – so therefore it didn't exist. I didn't need another reminder of them, as the weight of them and the impact on my small frame confirmed that they were still very much there. Daydreaming of better days was imperative for self-preservation.

We both hope that you enjoy this book but also learn something along the way. We've given what we can, now take what you need and feel free to laugh, cry and sing, at every step, we did.

1

Motherhood and All That Jazz

At the end of my twenties, a decade filled with new jobs, new friends, and a new husband, I knew perfectly well that I wanted to have children. I considered myself ready and able, confident of being that mother who knew exactly what to do; be kind and caring, administering discipline when necessary. Obviously, though, my children would always behave well and achieve all those milestones at the right time, if not even a bit earlier. I was, to say the least, naive to the seismic, earth-shattering effects of these little bundles of joy and the cost, both mentally and physically of motherhood.

No birthing plan or scheming can really prepare you for childbirth. Yes, you may want to give birth in a bath, put baby on breast then have Dad cut the cord, or even have a string quartet playing a fanfare of music to welcome your baby, but, in reality, at the end of it all, it happens in a process of its own, irrespective of the requirements of parents and all their carefully formulated paperwork. Our daughter's arrival into the world could not be planned for and was not in the usual way. She wore my amniotic sac like a veil around her head, causing my friend who was also my midwife, to gasp in surprise, "I have never seen anything like that before; I've heard about it but not seen it." She was referring, I later found out, to what is called an en caul birth, my waters hadn't broken so out she popped, with a great deal of effort from me, gift-wrapped in a shroud. Should I have taken this as an omen?

Well, apparently not, it is very rare, 1 in 80,000 births, auspicious and considered to be lucky. No need to worry, then. So, there was my daughter in the middle of two boys. A middle-born child, I have read, doesn't have the rights of the oldest or the privileges of the youngest but is lucky enough to have a syndrome.

As an organised mother, I began this job well equipped with Dr Miriam Stoppard's baby and child health book, a bible for all newbie mothers. This would, I was convinced, absolutely prepare me for all the myriad childhood illnesses or problems that accompany having children. Chicken pox, Ellen was covered from head to foot in spots, and she was even generous enough to pass it on to the boys. Allergies and asthma, pages galore in my bible, are chronic, long-term health conditions that may not have a cure. I was constantly finding foods that she would sick up, react to or just refuse to eat. Dust caused her to wheeze, so under duress, I felt obligated to hoover and dust regularly.

At the age of two, Ellen suffered several attacks of febrile convulsions. If you have never experienced a child who is having convulsions, let me tell you it is incredibly shocking and extremely worrying, and according to Dr Stoppard, it is dramatic and frightening but not life-threatening. That's a relief.

Picking her up, a dead weight in my arms, she was crying half-heartedly, the smell of sick wafting up from her little body, having vomited all over herself just as the plane landed. I struggled to put her coat on, and it was like time had stood still. I vaguely tried to make sense of what was happening, her crying had stopped and suddenly she shivered, shook, and convulsed in my arms. Horrified, feeling sick to my stomach, as her eyes began to roll and she lost consciousness, I truly thought she was going to die.

Although I don't remember getting there, we found ourselves in the baggage reclaim area, surrounded by airport staff who leapt into action. A space was cleared to lay her on the floor and an ambulance called. She felt so clammy to the touch and her little heart was beating at a rate of knots. As I carefully undid her coat, thoughts were swirling around my head. I was convinced she wasn't going to live through this. Not that I had any clue what 'this' was, I'd never seen anything like it before. Her Dad and brother hovered around, everyone at a loss as to know what was happening and how to help. I didn't take my eyes off her, watching, worrying and wondering what was to follow.

Gradually she stopped twitching, her eyes became more focussed on her surroundings, and I was just about able to breathe again. It felt like I hadn't taken a breath since the whole awful episode began, which was all of five minutes ago.

What's surprising is how nosey people are. There seemed to be people constantly lingering around, watching, and asking ridiculous questions and expecting me to reply.

"Please, if you are not medically trained, go away and stop gawping!" I pleaded. "What makes people come and stare when they know they cannot be of any help? Just move on. Go away! Vamoose! Clear Off!"

It was chaos; people stopping to stare, me frightened out of my life, heavily pregnant, convinced she was going to die, my husband and son helplessly looking on and the three emergency services simultaneously turning up. Realising that there wasn't a great deal the firemen could do they left but the police and the paramedics remained. Shaken to the core, very aware that we were centre stage to a drama unravelling in the airport, I was, thankfully, eventually taken with my daughter, who was placed on a stretcher, to the waiting ambulance while my husband took her brother and all the luggage back home. We were whisked off amidst flashing lights and sirens to the nearest hospital with suspected epilepsy, a diagnosis given by the paramedics. This was completely out of the blue. While she had been a bit poorly on holiday, with a runny nose, watery eyes and generally out of sorts, there'd been no hint there was anything so dramatic on the horizon.

I had to stay overnight with her, which wasn't the most comfortable when you're in a child's bed and you're six months pregnant. We didn't have a change of clothes and the smell of sick seemed to be on everything I touched. No matter, we were in the right place and that's all that I cared about.

Fortunately, epilepsy was an incorrect diagnosis and doctors confirmed that she had actually suffered a febrile convulsion. I was told that these are caused by the body's inability to regulate the body temperature and had been triggered by an ear infection. Oh, how pleased I was! The fact that the diagnosis was not an ongoing condition was such a relief. I do remember her feeling so very hot against me, but when you're pregnant being hot is par for the course and I didn't think anything of it. Apparently, keeping her cool rather than covering her up with her coat, as I had when we left the plane, would have been a lot more helpful. You live and learn.

Once the antibiotics for the ear infection began to work, the fits stopped, and life gradually returned to normal. She never suffered from them after that and I was told, quite correctly, that by the time she reached four or five they would stop.

Ellen continued to keep me on my toes. To be honest there really has never been a dull moment in her life and her early years at school reflected this. She struggled to read or write, definitely not reaching the expected attainment levels. I ended up going in to see the Head Teacher with my concerns who at that time, wasn't too worried.

"They'll all get there in their own time." These very flippant words were said to me in 2001 when she was six years old, and I now know that this is a completely inaccurate fact. If a child has dyslexia, which we subsequently discovered my daughter had, they will not, 'get there', unless specialist intervention is put in place.

We were eventually told that because of her dyslexia, it would be difficult to support her at this fee-paying school, so we had to move her. Let me get this straight; she doesn't fight with the other children, isn't rude, doesn't cause a problem in the classroom, is always on time and her parents have never defaulted on paying the fees, her only crime is that she is struggling to learn in the same way or pace as most of the children. Had the teaching profession lost its raison d'etre?

An interesting comment she made to me when she was old

enough to understand, was that when she was sitting in the classroom, she was always in a constant state of worry and uncertainty about what was expected of her, what she had to do and to avoid this, she would simply daydream away her day. As any mother can imagine this made me sad for her and angry about the lack of understanding on the part of this educational establishment.

Then there was the pitter-patter of little feet coming to tell me she had wet the bed.

"Really? Not again," I groaned. "Why is it you just can't wake up and go to the toilet? This is happening three or four times a week."

Falling out of bed, half asleep, tiptoeing around, I grudgingly changed the sheets and her with as little disruption as possible. I would kiss my daughter good night again and stumble back to bed, waiting to be claimed by sleep but knowing full well that I would now be wide awake until morning.

Bed wetting or enuresis is extremely common in young children but knowing this fact didn't make it any easier. I tried everything that Miriam had suggested but it was happening so frequently, and it was annoying, frustrating, and exhausting. I did feel a tiny bit guilty for getting angry with her over something that I knew she was probably unable to control. But guilt, I soon realised, went hand in hand with being a mother. A trip to the doctor's surgery was the next step. We were referred to the children's clinic and after explaining the problem I came away armed with the medication, Vasopressin, which had been prescribed by the clinician. I was feeling confident that this would be the answer to my little girl's bed-wetting problems.

Vasopressin is a man-made form of an anti-diuretic hormone, (ADH) which is secreted by the pituitary gland. It works by decreasing water excretion from the kidneys. Over the next couple of days, it worked its magic and the bed-wetting stopped. This result was not only good for my sleep deprivation but also for my daughter too. Unfortunately, and all too frequently as I soon found out, life gives with one hand and takes with the other. After only a short time of being prescribed these tablets, I was seriously alarmed when she began to produce a vaginal discharge; shocked, to say the least, and surprised by this, as she was still so young. I decided immediately that a week into using this medication, it was just too much of a coincidence to think there wasn't a link between these tablets and what could be considered early puberty, to my little girl who was just nine years of age and very slight of build. They were stopped forthwith.

The question is, could these tablets have affected her in more ways than anyone knew? There were no recorded side effects that I could find and when I did mention it to people in the medical profession, it was of no consequence or little importance; puberty was going to happen anyway.

Ellen had her fair share of bucking the rules, not following the norm and generally going it alone and motherhood hadn't necessarily panned out as I had imagined. But overall, up to the tender age of ten, my daughter developed normally and there were no obvious signs, apart from the discharge which had only occurred once, of early puberty, precocious puberty, or any other puberty. Her body seemed to be going to plan. It was really in the summer of 2006 at age eleven that there were signs that her breasts had started to grow but nothing else and I suppose I thought that this was early but inevitable. According to the NHS website, the average age for girls to begin puberty is eleven, so I didn't feel there was anything really to be concerned about.

I made a decision not to worry about this early onset of breast growth. Let's face it, so far in her short life, she hadn't been a child known to follow what was expected or necessarily the norm. So, just before her eleventh birthday, we went out and bought a bra to acknowledge her budding breasts, rather than hide them. She recalls feeling quite excited about buying this A-cup bra with its polka-dot burgundy spots. Nobody else in her year had begun to wear bras and she recollects the feeling of being girly and feminine. But as she so vividly recalls, this situation was short-lived:

Suddenly they grew so quickly with not a lot of time in between, I really didn't know what was happening.

No sooner had we bought her this bra and she was happily wearing it, than within a month the bra no longer fitted, and she had not just slightly outgrown it but hugely outgrown it.

It is impossible not to compare your own daughter to friends' children and it was so obvious that she was the only one who had started to develop breasts. What I remember was fervently wishing that she had the same shaped body as her friends, who were very slowly developing as they should. I couldn't understand why it was that with her small frame she was growing breasts that simply didn't fit or make sense. No matter how I looked at it there seemed no logic in it at all; her height and weight didn't add up to her breast size, which was not age-appropriate. Despite my mounting unease, in my mind, I had persuaded myself that this growth spurt was completely normal and that her friends would catch up in no time.

This was not the case. The very worrying realisation was the speed at which her breasts began to grow. From the summer of 2006 to the beginning of January 2007, they had developed quite dramatically, and it was becoming plainly obvious to me and to her, that this surely couldn't be normal. Alarm bells were ringing, albeit in the distance, but with every month that went by those bells gradually became louder.

What followed, in the wake of this very first bra purchase, must surely be one of the most overriding, uncomprehending, indescribably, and psychologically damaging childhood diseases of all, one that had the medical profession scratching their heads and which sent our family life into a downward, spinning spiral.

2

How Big is Too Big?

"And so I wake in the morning
And I step outside
And I take a deep breath and I get real high
And I scream from the top of my lungs
"What's going on?"

Diary extract, 8th February 2007:

We've got Ellen's first appointment with the Doctor today, regarding her unusual breast growth. I've been told to take her height and weight and bring this information along to the appointment. I have no idea what he will say nor whether he will think there is anything wrong. I'm absolutely certain that her breast size is not right, and I have this guilty feeling that maybe it was the Vasopressin tablets. I don't know for sure, so we'll just have to wait and see.

Encouraging and cajoling your children up in the morning to arrive at school, fed, watered, on time and with everything they need, is bad enough but when that child, metaphorically speaking, has a pair of weights strapped to her chest, it can only be described as a struggle against adversity. I would pause outside her bedroom door, take a deep breath, put a big smile on my face and in I'd go.

"Time to get up, wakey-wakey." At this point, I tended to hold my breath to see what further damage her body had inflicted on her during the night.

"Do I have to get up and go to school? I'm just too tired and

I think they've grown again." Looking down awkwardly, she sounded so miserable and depressed and as lying on her front was far too difficult and uncomfortable, she lay there on her back, peering down at her chest to see the changes that had happened almost overnight. She was right.

I was working on keeping my emotional responses on an even keel.

"Um, a little maybe. You know, one day I'll come into your bedroom, and I won't be able to see you because they will be touching the ceiling! Come on, it will be sorted, don't worry, you won't be like this for long." I reassured her with fingers, toes and everything else crossed.

We both laughed half-heartedly but actually inside I was silently screaming. I was well aware that it wasn't me who had to deal with the daily physical grind of getting up, putting on parts of her school uniform that still fitted her, cobbling together the rest and then walking to the school bus with these large and still growing appendages. As well as the ridicule and comments, "What you got stuffed up your jumper?" "You know, the girl with the big tits."

This was the pattern of most weekday mornings. She was reluctant to go to school for obvious reasons, but I was insistent that she went. So, I would encourage, coax and do my very best to get her out of the door. This is how she remembers it:

After being woken up I would just lay there until Mum use to shout at me from the bottom of the stairs, telling me to get up. I'm not really a morning person at the best of times. I just didn't have the energy, my body was unable to move, with my heavy chest and probably an unrecognisable amount of depression – I just wanted to evaporate and not face the world anymore, and Mum was needing me to go and get the bus. Having these morning screaming matches, I could have done without. It was just so difficult. I would reluctantly get dressed, drag my feet up the hill and on occasions miss the bus, so I would have to get the train which required even more effort – but at least that ate into my school day.

I just didn't want to go. Every day at school was testing; either I'd get told off because my tie was a millimetre out of place or not the correct shape and always with an audience of my rowdy peer group. Or I would feel really sad because as much as I'd tried to cover up my huge chest, somebody, including teachers, would say something to make me feel painfully awkward and embarrassed, inferring I'd got something stuffed up my top and to 'take it out', and then watching the horror on their face when they realised, they'd got it wrong. A good day would consist of no one acknowledging or even addressing me at all – but the trade-off for humiliation was loneliness – and I'm not sure which one was worse.

I stood waving goodbye, watching her disappear, reluctantly, around the corner. It was so hard sending her out of the front door knowing that she was excruciatingly self-conscious of the person she was rapidly becoming and too young to understand the woman that they had prematurely turned her into. How many times had I wished that it could all go away, and she would be a young eleven-year-old girl, looking forward to becoming a beautiful, normal shape, teenage girl? Instead of which, the top half of her body resembled the physical appearance of a page three model.

Did she have a disability? Yes, she did, but was it recognised? No, it was not on anybody's radar.

On many occasions I had a lot of, 'what if' thoughts and one of these was, what if I could bottle this disease and sell it to all those women who from choice go under the knife to have exactly what we were struggling to get rid of? The British Association of Aesthetic Plastic Surgery reveal that the UK's most popular plastic surgery is breast augmentation (enlargement), and this is also true in America. The 2018 Plastic Surgery Statistics Report from the American Society of Plastic Surgeons notes that breast augmentation has been the top-ranking cosmetic procedure in the USA since 2006. Imagine how much money we could make, I would fantasise about what we could do with it. If only our minds could shape our reality, I would be a rich woman. It was a very short-lived dream and the true reality, unfortunately, had to be faced.

On February 8th, 2007, at the young age of eleven years, she had an initial appointment with our family doctor, who agreed that perhaps they were slightly large, B/C cup, which wasn't too big but big enough for her age and size. She was 1m 47cm tall and weighed 6 stone. The blood tests encouragingly showed that there were no abnormal levels of oestrogen, and it was agreed that we would be referred to a female Paediatric Consultant, (my request), in our local hospital. Unfortunately, this appointment wasn't until August 2007, a further six months later. And no one was prepared for the damage that her body could inflict in such a short time.

By the end of the summer of 2007 and at the start of the school term, her breasts had grown six sizes larger, to an alarming and enormous size G-cup. They were growing almost according to the months; with every month that went by, her size would surely follow. Returning to school wasn't any fun at all for her. The size she was made even simple activities very difficult; her situation was becoming intolerable. The thought of how big they could become was far too depressing to think about.

They were not only difficult to deal with but weren't a pleasant sight. The skin over her breasts was so stretched, taut and transparent, with the blue of her veins showing through, they hung like pendulums and the nipples no longer protruded like nipples but were flat and diminished. These could no longer, under any circumstances, be considered a girl's breasts; they had become a hugely distorted and uncomprehending version of them.

In the meantime, however, life had to go on and this meant her life at school, swimming, ballet, friends, and the normal activities of a young, healthy girl. This was the problem though, while she was not quite so active, she was healthy in a way that didn't require medical intervention, at least not yet. But as Ellen said herself, her mental health was suffering and I was, I'm sorry to say, to begin with, more aware of her physical state than her mental state. It was difficult for anybody to understand or believe what she and we as a family were going through. No matter how hard family and friends tried to understand, unless they'd been through it, they just couldn't comprehend what it was like and understand fully the emotional challenges, fears and mental struggles that were with her every day.

There seemed to be no one out there who had experienced this or was experiencing it. No reputable website, support groups or charities, meant no camaraderie from fellow mothers or parents, which I was badly in need of and most of all nobody to whom my daughter could relate. The very last thing you wanted to do was Google, 'large breast'. This produced a variety of websites that were neither appropriate nor of any help whatsoever and not what I wanted to look at; not in the least. In fact, I did think that if for some reason my computer had to be taken away, the history on its hard drive would make interesting viewing. When I was brave enough to type in, 'large breasts', from the depths of the internet, I discovered the following; seriously, how I laughed to the point of tears! Is it possible that there are people out there who really believe this?

"*How can I grow my breasts in 2 days?*

It's simple!

1. *Add oestrogen-rich foods to your everyday diet. (Apple, Fenugreek seeds, olive oil, oranges, peaches, dairy products, walnuts, ginger, peanuts etc.)*
2. *Regular breast massage. (Increases production of prolactin, a hormone that is responsible for breast enlargement).*
3. *Drink dandelion root tea every day.*

Friends and family rallied around and any information that they thought would be useful was passed on. In fact, I was given an article entitled, 'Why I cut off my girl's breasts'. This was a true story of a fifteen-year-old girl whose breasts grew so disproportionately, that she had to have a breast reduction. Although it was a similar story, the girl was four years older, and not as big at the time of her operation, as Ellen was at this moment in time. Nevertheless, it was still a harrowing account of a young girl dealing with similar issues. Overall, though, we were struggling on our own with a very cruel and as yet nameless disease.

I appreciate that until you saw them, which was a societal obstacle, it's not something we reveal or even discuss openly, it was difficult to have an understanding. A broken limb, measles, or appendicitis can be understood, sympathised and empathised with, and even books written to give support with these illnesses, but large boobs, not at all. They are the butt of people's jokes, seedy and unwanted and the cause of numerous stares, which put together are a violation of women's rights, let alone a young girl's.

Her time spent at school was by no means easy and I wish I could say that the school was understanding, supportive and aware of her needs but that just wasn't the case, even though I had been in to explain the situation and written a letter. Let me tell you, explaining your daughter's rapidly growing breasts to a male Head Teacher was frankly embarrassing for both of us. I felt that through my inability to communicate this problem sufficiently, I had let my daughter down as well as the whole female race. I was desperate to have a different problem to talk to him about than this. I stuttered, explained as efficiently as I could and said that she was coping well, and it would all be sorted.

What was I thinking? NO, we weren't coping well, and NO nothing at that time was being sorted. Why did I say this? I realised that what I was trying to do was normalising the abnormal. It was simply too difficult for me to be honest. The results of my poor communication skills and his lack of understanding resulted in not a lot happening in terms of providing a safe and caring environment, which she so badly needed. Schools have a duty to ensure the physical and emotional welfare of your child. This Head Teacher reasoned that singling her out and providing extra pastoral care would ultimately leave her feeling different and vulnerable. I wonder how he thought she felt when on one occasion Ellen was late for a lesson. She entered the classroom and apologised for being late, whereupon the teacher proceeded to ask her what she had stuffed up her jumper. What the-? This teacher, I can only assume, had no knowledge of my daughter's issue. Otherwise, knowing her condition, why would you say this to her or for that matter any young girl? With that Ellen turned tail and ran to the toilets where she burst into tears.

To this day, I still don't know what to make of this appalling behaviour. Where were the care and support? Where was the Head Teacher's pastoral care and more to the point, the communication ensuring that all the teachers understand each and every child? Seriously sucks. It wasn't just some of the teachers that proved to be unbelievably ignorant but there was also a very real difficulty in finding school uniforms that fitted. The aprons, bibs and science lab coats required by the school, also posed a real problem for her; she was simply too big to wear them. Embarrassing or what? Did the school help? No. Did I go in and complain? I'm afraid not. Time was critical: time at work, time trying to look after the family and home, time attending to my daughter's needs and last but not least, time chasing hospital appointments and test results. I had no time to make complaints about teachers, who should know better. Old Father Time had me well and truly in his grip. To say I was in a constant state of anxiety, was an understatement. I was so desperately trying to support her as much as possible with what little information I had and feeling so very sad about the difficult life she was leading.

My heart also went out to her brothers, who, by being at the same school, had to experience and see for themselves the reactions of teachers and students and the very tricky life she had to negotiate and navigate to hide the rapid and excessive growth of her breasts. From January onwards, when they took off, her life became undeniably difficult and as a result, so too did theirs.

Hindsight is a wonderful thing, but I wonder whether I was right to make her go to school, to walk out of the front door and be subjected to the cruel and mean jibes that are the school playground and it would seem the school classroom. Did I do the right thing by being that bad-ass mum who said to her daughter that life must go on, up you get, and you can't just roll over, not that rolling anywhere was an option, and give in? Should I have given up work and taught her at home? It didn't occur to me at the time to home-school her; was I right or wrong? I just don't know. What difference would it have made if she simply hadn't gone to school but worked from home for the duration of her illness? That, however, was the crux of the matter; how long was this situation going to go on and how big would they grow? We simply had no idea. It was anybody's guess.

The fact is, I did usher her out of the door in the mornings and I did tell her that life must go on. From my daughter's perspective, staying at home would have been more comfortable, safe and free from external trials and tribulations but as she said:

'It wouldn't have been right. You can't hide yourself away from society as it has negative implications; it's not good for those that judge or those that are judged. The fewer people that are visible with their deformities the less we understand and accept them.

These were Ellen's brave words, said when she was older, insightful words indeed. It was her summing up of my attempt at normality, at trying to carry on with life, no matter what. Much to my relief she also said that going to school made it easier for her to appreciate College where she could make a new start.

Clothes were a minefield, forget fashion. Anything that would fit attractively on the top half of her, would swim on the rest of her, looking like she had borrowed a very big sister's outfit. Finding bras to fit was hard enough, but swimming costumes became a thing of the past. Swimwear was a cobbled-together mix of big bras and bikini bottoms with a huge t-shirt over the top. Her attitude was 'Cover them up and desperately hope no one notices'.

There was one particularly awkward occasion in a well-known, young person's trendy shop on Oxford Street, 'Top Shop', that stopped any further shopping sprees for good. It happened just as her size was becoming far too unmanageable. It was busy and very hot in the store and after queuing to pay, I headed back to Ellen. I found her leaning against a rail, looking grey and drawn, having a full-blown panic attack, complaining of feeling hot, sick, racing heart and dizziness.

"Let's take off your jacket and allow yourself to cool down a bit." This was probably making the situation worse; she was carrying a lot of weight around. She still had her jacket on and the shop was mobbed and all these bodies were probably providing enough heat to light up the whole of Oxford Street.

"Stay there, while I find somewhere to sit."

Trying not to panic, I hastily approached a shop assistant and explained the situation. She kindly took us into a room at the back of the store, offered us some water and left us in peace. Neither of us wanted any fuss and were more than happy just to sit there until she had calmed down. However, the kindly assistant, who was only doing her job, informed her manager, who promptly stepped into action. He became involved and thinking this was the right thing to do, called the Paramedics. Oh Lordy. Did he have to do that? We were fine, she was fine, leave us alone and we'll go quietly. For a girl and a mother who didn't want to attract drama, this was rapidly becoming one.

"Mum, I'm feeling better now, shall we just go, leave while we can?"

"Oh, my goodness, I think it's too late. It will look really odd if we get up and walk out now. Oh great, they're here!"

The paramedics arrived looking professionally concerned and keen to do what their job entailed; check her over, listen to her heart and more than likely do various other tests. But let me put it into perspective, this happened at a time when her breasts were very large. I don't think they had reached J-cup but not far off it. My daughter had become adept at hiding their size beneath her jacket or whatever top she was wearing. To remove another layer of clothing in front of them was most definitely, without a doubt, not an option. The paramedics, understandably, wanted to do their job properly, which I understood but this was not a normal situation. My daughter was not what they were expecting, and I could see this becoming very awkward and embarrassing for all concerned. I simply had no words of explanation; I was beyond trying to explain her situation to anyone. It hadn't gone well with the Head Teacher at her school and I didn't want to try again even with medical professionals. I doubted if there was anybody who would understand.

How I managed to stop these very enthusiastic and professional medics from giving her a thorough check, I just don't know. My daughter looked scared stiff. Her earlier symptoms had vanished, and she was ready to run. I was flustered and rambled on about how she was fully recovered, and it was essential that we left now because we had an important appointment, not really, but I had to say something. Forgive me for telling little white lies but sometimes they're essential. Seriously, I think in the end it was me they considered needed to be checked over mentally, locked up and the key thrown away, which actually wasn't a bad idea.

We left this room, the Paramedics and this High Street shop as soon as it was physically possible and essentially before my daughter was asked to take off her top. We backed out of the door at the same time as reassuring them that she was absolutely fine, thanking them for their concern and please, please, please could they let us go? As soon as it was possible, we both walked and half-ran right out of the shop. We probably looked more like shop lifters than normal shoppers. Normal, however, just didn't come into it. It's not difficult to see now, why shopping causes us both to go into panic mode.

Life, very sadly, had become just that, a state of constant

panic. It was too difficult for Ellen to deal with. We were completely in the dark as to what was happening to her, and there was no doubt that her situation and her size were getting worse by the month.

3

BRAving the Storm

And I say, "Hey-ey-ey-ey"
Hey-ey-ey
I said, "Hey, what's going on?"

Diary extract, a Saturday in May 2007, 11 years old:

I didn't look forward to this day at all. It was essential that she had some properly fitting bras, or as I remember from my school days, a derogatory name, an over-the-shoulder boulder holder. Where would we get them and how easy it would be, left a big question mark. What size we would need to buy was just going to be a guess. I hadn't, however, bargained for the sales assistant to be so God damn rude.

"So how old are you, then, dear?" asked the rather nosy shop assistant, as she bundled into the changing rooms, arms full of bras. Ellen was in the middle of extracting herself from one that was far too small and was angry with me because I was, obviously, of no help and why had I given her such a small size?

Neither of us said anything and all I could think was Oh, for goodness sakes, does she have to gawp like that? Is she one of those insensitive creatures that have no qualms about staring at other people's disabilities? Absolutely none of your business how old she is, that's what, and you're never likely to win the company's diplomacy award, or any other customer service award for that matter. Was this question about age necessary and relevant to our shopping requirements? Isn't it just the correct size and fit, for that all-important support they need to get right? Age shouldn't come into it.

Here we were in one very well-known high street shop, Marks and Spencer, trying our best, which amounted to an inconceivably difficult struggle, to buy a bra that would be comfortable, fit well and provide support. Unfortunately, her lovely pink, spotted, dotty A-cup bra, which we had bought under such different circumstances, so easily and pleasantly, had been pushed to the back of the drawer. She had worn it for as long as it was physically possible and then she had resorted to sports bras, but even these were becoming redundant as they gave very little support and just weren't large enough.

For nearly an hour, although it seemed much longer, we had trawled through all the stands and racks of bras on display. It was confusing, to say the least, to know what size to choose and as for worrying about colour and trend, that was a luxury and just wasn't an option. Eventually, having gone around one too many times looking at the same bras, we took a selection of sizes and styles into the changing rooms, but we had chosen badly as there was just nothing that would fit. Every bra she tried on just wasn't doing its job, too small, too tight, and even too big but just simply didn't fit. The atmosphere in the changing room was becoming a little charged and overheated, to say the least, and we were both becoming agitated and frustrated with this hopeless situation. I finally and reluctantly decided to request some assistance, which was something I had tried to avoid, not wanting to put Ellen, myself, or the assistant in a difficult or embarrassing situation. I did, however, expect someone who wasn't going to be intrusive by asking unnecessary questions and who had a modicum of integrity with some initiative to know when and what to say and when it was best to remain silent. Unfortunately, this assistant turned out to be none of the above and she just wasn't a person either of us needed at that time.

After a fraught and frazzled half hour where we tried on any number of bras, it was obvious that we weren't going to be able to make a purchase in this shop. My heart truly sank at the thought of having to spend another couple of hours trudging from shop to shop, dealing with inappropriate comments only to come away not having bought anything, finding that nothing would fit.

"I'm afraid we just don't have any that will fit your shape; it may be best to try a specialist shop."

Thanks for nothing, I could have worked that one out myself. I was pleasantly surprised, though, that she said 'shape' and not 'size'. It slightly eased my feeling of wanting to stab her. I do sound like a rather bad-tempered customer but she must have seen that this was a really awkward situation, especially for my daughter. On impulse, I wanted to tell her that it was bad customer service to ask questions that would most probably cause embarrassment to the customer and were not relevant to the purchase. I didn't though, for the simple reason that we both wanted to head right out of the door as quickly as possible, not look back and definitely not return. We were both feeling pretty much as though we had been put through the wringer.

"Can we just go home now and not bother? I don't really care what I wear."

Yes, these were my sentiments too but, "We'll go to one more shop and if we can't find anything we'll head home."

"Seriously, I'm really tired, fed up and hungry and what's the point?"

"Right, one more shop and then we'll go to get something to eat and head home. Come on, we're nearly there."

The point was she knew as well as I did that it was very important to find a well-fitting bra, so she grudgingly agreed, and we continued our weary way.

The very real problem concerning shopping for bras, when you are aged eleven going on twelve and a size E-cup, is that there is little or, as we found out, no demand for this size cup with a 26" chest/rib cage. She had a narrow, small frame and the body of a young girl except for these gigantic mammary glands. The term 'mammary glands' is medically known as the breasts located on the front of the chest. I quite like the name because it contains less of a sexual connotation and helps to avoid repeating the word breasts all the time.

Empty-handed and still bristling with indignation we went on with our search. Standing outside a possible shop, we both felt a slight reluctance to go in, feeling almost embarrassed like naughty girls, having been burnt by our previous retail experience. Our feelings, thank goodness, were unfounded and they were so much more helpful and although I could tell the shop assistant, was a little surprised, nothing was said and she didn't utter a single, inappropriate word. Yes, that's the way to do it. This eased the situation greatly, I just really cared for my daughter's feelings and another insensitive assistant was at best going to hurt and at worst possibly have put her, or both of us off shopping for what was an essential garment. It was impossible for her not to wear any support at all and so it was imperative that we bought at least one on this shopping trip.

Thankfully, we came away with two bras and I was going to buy a third when it occurred to me that the chance of her growth stopping didn't seem very likely and to buy another one the same size and one which would probably not fit in the weeks to come, was a waste. I thought it best to stick with two and see how the situation with her size unfolded as the days went on. We didn't care or have a choice as to the colour or style; we were just grateful to find two that fitted comfortably and gave her that all-important support. It was a great result and such a positive achievement. At least now we knew where we would most likely be able to make this difficult purchase again, without too much awkwardness, Bravissimo.

The other problem, as I had predicted, was that these visits to what, in the end, had to be to specialist shops specialising in sizes that weren't run of the mill, were practically every month. It was a nerve-wracking, humiliating and soul-destroying visit. Bras that fitted were not the pretty, delicate, fashion-contoured, garment, (like her pink, spotty dotty bra), which is what you're really looking to buy for a young girl but more heavy-duty, weight-bearing instruments of practicality and a great deal more expensive.

From January 2007 through to her first Paediatric Consultant's appointment in August of the same year, her breasts had grown from a size B-cup to an E-cup. By the time we had our very first Paediatric consultation, life for her was desperate and all she wanted was to get rid of them and that's all I wanted for her, too. There are many things that you may wish or want for your daughter, a breast reduction isn't something that springs to mind but what was the alternative? What choice did we have? A life that revolved around the continued growth of her breasts, backache, chest pains, shoulder ache, embarrassment, difficulty in buying clothes, inability to run and even to have a bath required someone to hold and support them whilst she clambered in and out. Is that what you want for your nearest and dearest? I know what my answer was and still is.

The next page contains pictures of just a few of the bras we bought over a continuously unpleasant and drawn-out period of her life. There were many more, but I just decided on these few, maybe because they weren't so much her favourite as the most comfortable. Why did I hang on to them? I suppose they meant so much in so many different ways; they represented a great deal of heartache and emotion and to throw them away, to disregard them, just didn't feel right. Who knows, by the end of this book, my decision might change and I might not feel so attached to them. Ellen, on the other hand, can't bear to even look at them. To her, they are simply a reminder of a period in her short life that she would very much like to forget and bitterly regretted ever happening to her.

See for yourself the bra sizes that she was growing out of within a month or two and the sizes she had to deal with, between the ages of eleven and twelve years old. No age at all and certainly not an age to be dealing with the amount of breast tissue needed to fill such large-sized, over-the-shoulder boulder holders.

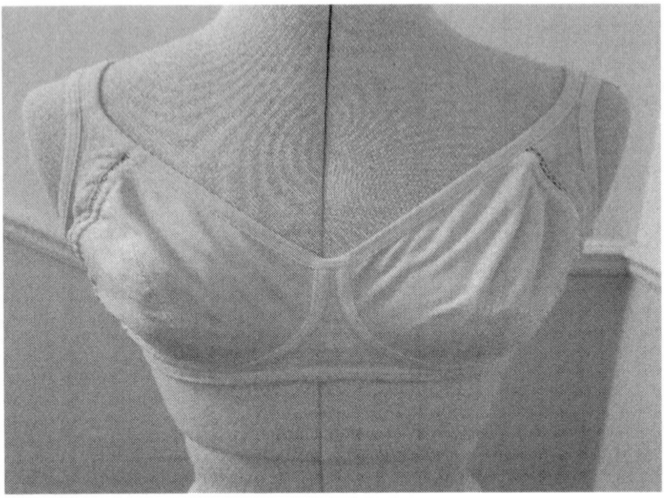

This bra is a Size D-cup and she wore this, aged 11.

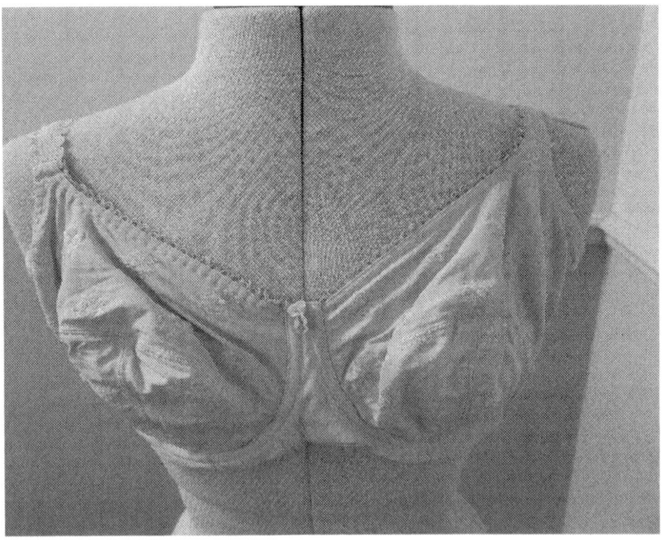

This is a size E-cup, at aged 11.

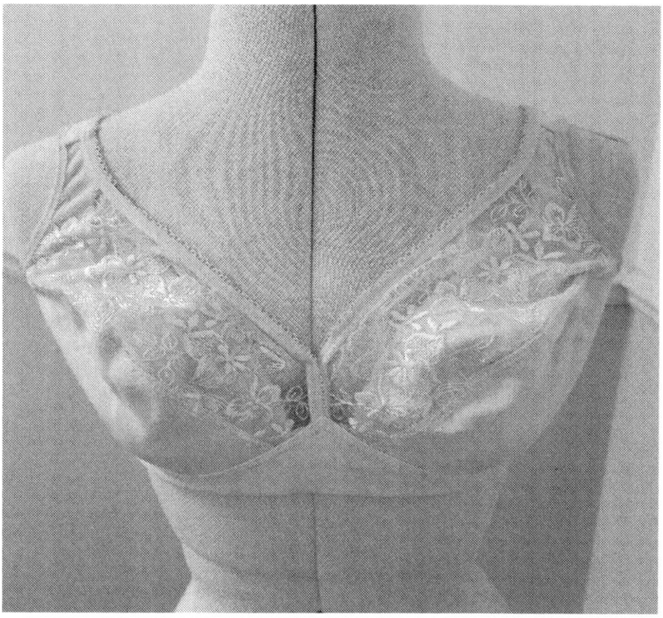

This is a Size F-cup she wore aged 12.

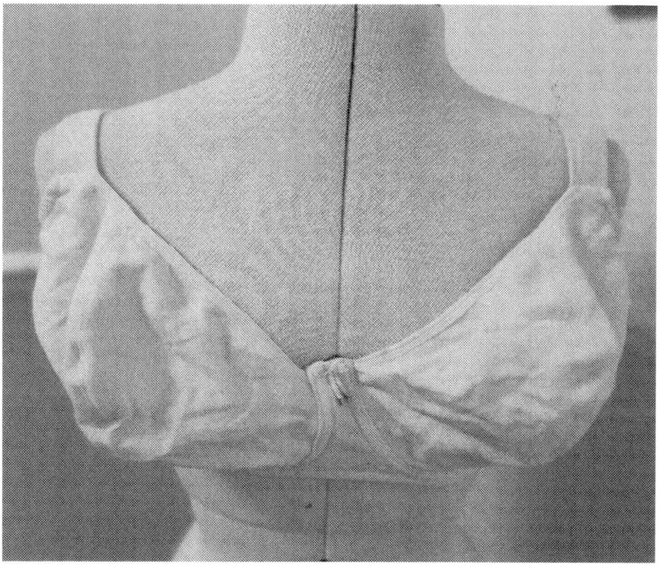

Size G/H-cup aged 12.

Size K-cup, aged 12.

Size L-cup, aged 12.

4

We're All Going on a Camping Holiday

"I realized quickly when I knew I should
That the world was made up of this brotherhood of man
For whatever that means."

Diary extract, July 2007:

A holiday, it would seem, with plenty of baggage.

"Oh, for goodness' sake Mum, will you please tell her to stop it, it's gross!"

"I really don't care what you think or anyone else, I am so hot and sweaty and I'm feeling really uncomfortable."

It was a scorching hot day and the French roads, as usual in the summer, were chaos. We were driving back to the campsite after a day spent exploring Spain's coastline. I was lost in thought listening to our standard choice of music, which comprised mainly of rock ballads. I think it was on this holiday that 'What's Up' became one of our favourites, although at this time it hadn't quite become our anthem. Shouting coming from the back of the car broke my train of thought, so I turned the music down and peered into the back, prepared to referee three irritable children. I was not expecting what I was confronted with and just had to laugh when I saw the cause of her brother's complaints. Their sister, in her own inimitable way, had stripped off to the waist and had lifted her breasts, naked and untethered onto the pull-down table at the back of the driver's seat. Not something you see every day and not something any of us, least of all me, knew how to deal with.

This was a very interesting situation for the boys. I knew it was incredibly awkward and embarrassing to see their sister display everything, even though they were aware of some of the difficulties she had. To them, it was not acceptable. However, I could only sympathise and understand wholeheartedly why she had manhandled herself into this position. The weather was thirty degrees and even with air conditioning, which I'm not sure was even working, the car was unbearably hot. To her they were not the breasts she had at ten years of age, they could just as well be lumps anywhere on her body and her actions meant nothing to her, it was simply a way of cooling off. To her brothers, on the other hand, they were still breasts, a part of the female anatomy that they were only just beginning to understand. A real dichotomy which required a sense of humour.

This time in Ellen's life was particularly difficult. Her breasts had grown and seemingly were continuing to grow to a size which would be considered large, for even a larger adult woman. Understandably, they were heavy and extremely hot to the touch. The summer's high temperatures in confined spaces weren't a good mix and so this was the result; two shocked and bad-tempered boys and an overheating young girl who had total disregard for convention.

As I took in the scene in the back of the car, I had to wonder how many other families had experienced this dilemma. All I could think of doing was to make light of it.

"Oh, my goodness, I just hope that passing cars and lorries, who will probably have a bird's eye view, don't cause a massive pile up on these busy French roads. How would they explain to the Gendarme the reasons for the accident? What we don't want is to be caught in a traffic jam, then I think it would be best to cover them up!"

"No mum, she needs to cover them up, now!"

"Look, for the time being, it's not offending anybody else.

Come on, it's not that bad."

But it was 'that bad' for the boys. I knew it was but what else could she do? They were massively - excuse the pun - uncomfortable. Should the boys have to witness what she was doing? I was momentarily at a loss as to how to deal with it. There wasn't a parenting or healthcare book in the world that could help me here. It was way beyond any advice Dr Miriam Stoppard could give.

However, I decided that sometimes life is about dealing with strange and unusual circumstances. And yes, they would have to accept what she was doing, just for the time being.

"Just carry on cooling off, until we're in another traffic jam or until we reach the campsite and then cover them up." Smiling at her as I said it and wishing to whatever deity was listening, that I knew what was happening to her body.

"Well, I'm not even going to look," complained her older brother.

"That's fine you don't need to, look out of the window at the lovely scenery."

It wasn't fair to tell her off; she hadn't done anything wrong. Nor was it reasonable, for the time being anyway, to tell her to cover them up. Here was a problem with no right or wrong answers. We laughed; well, the boys struggled with this, and she continued to rest and cool her excess baggage on the table.

Camping on the Southwest coast of France was a great holiday. It's a beautiful part of the country with a stunning coastline and the weather is always reliable, a real plus when camping. It was the height of summer, and we could surf, body-board and swim with a long expanse of sandy beach to sit on. It was preferrable to the campsite's pool. This was particularly so for Ellen, because sitting around a busy communal pool, or even swimming in a busy pool, could be fraught with insecurities. It seems that everyone looks at everyone else and it gave her an awful feeling of being exposed and of being on show. So, she tended to remain at the beach, which was not much better. She was still subjected to scrutiny by idiots who, quite obviously, didn't know any better. People, however, SHOULD know better.

Bodyboarding, surfing and attempting to swim are all fun but by ten o'clock in the morning, there wasn't a grain of sand left to sit down on. It seemed like the whole of France was here and the coastline was packed. From the start, it was obvious that our time spent on the beach caused some unnecessary stares, especially from overweight, red-faced, middle-aged men. Biased on my part, yes but it was true. She didn't like walking down to the sea on her own, so one of us would go with her and it was difficult to try and pretend that she wasn't being stared at. Donning my invisible armour hoping to protect Ellen against awkward stares, we'd head off down to the sea. Thrusting our shoulders back; actually, I was the one doing that, and she was doing her best to hide what was proving difficult to ignore. We walked with an attitude and tried to give the impression of nonchalance; sticks and stones and all that. It was a bit like running the gauntlet; we were kind of on public trial. Once we reached the sea, she was relatively safe from prying eyes. What I found incredible was that people didn't even have the decency to pretend not to look, devoid of any common courtesy. Perhaps because we were in France, people like to stare more, I don't know, would it have happened on a UK beach? Yes, probably.

Unfortunately, human nature is such that anything out of the ordinary, that doesn't comply with the normal map, encourages people to stop and look and ask questions. Had she been larger limbed, taller framed then maybe this wouldn't have happened, but the fact was, here was a girl who had just turned twelve years old and looked it, had a small frame but had the most unfortunate luck to have enormous breasts. She was literally the cause of so many stares. This twelve-year-old was well aware of the looks and not even wearing one of her heavy-duty bras with a baggy t-shirt over the top, prevented them.

It wasn't even as if she was sitting in the car displaying all. Then I might have understood the rude ogling and gaping that was happening around us. To be honest, it made me realise how our culture has become more sexualised through social media, fashion and advertising and that children have become the casualties of adult exploitation. My daughter was no exception. She was being sexually objectified when childhood should be a time of innocence. She quite literally grew up too fast.

We tried to shrug this problem off, accepting that there were worse things that could happen, but the truth be told, it hurt, and there were many times she would go back to the tent in tears. It was times like these that really tested my ability to stay calm; I could quite easily have burst into tears with her. But I had to remain positive, telling her that the situation will change; she won't be like this forever. Reminding her that we had an appointment with the Paediatric Consultant at the end of August and let's try to ignore these people who were obviously ignorant and ill-mannered. She listened but for a young girl of twelve when all she wanted to do was join her brothers in the sea or the pool, without feeling she was the source of unwanted attention and interest, was very difficult to accept.

I felt awful for her and would have readily thrown sand in the face of anyone who even looked in her direction. Were they aware of what happens when a person gets between a mother bear and her cubs? Apparently not. However, it just wasn't the right thing to do. I still had two boys who were, so far, innocently oblivious to this and I wanted it to remain that way.

I did take them to one side and just remind them of how her situation, at the moment, was not pleasant for her and to be a little understanding and that it would all get sorted. They listened but whether they truly understood or could empathise was doubtful. Puberty for them hadn't even started so understanding this situation with their sister was a big ask. It had happened, it was still happening, this was the fact and they accepted it. Their little lives had to carry on regardless. What else could be said?

As for the onlookers, I just didn't think that turning into a raving, maniacal, sand-throwing mother would help in any way. Although I wanted to scream out to stop them from objectifying my daughter by gawping at her anomalous body. It, perhaps, would have made me feel better. My needs, though, were way down on that pecking order list.

Our days on holiday were fun and although they weren't completely carefree, they were at least a change of scenery with the ability to take part in different activities and most of all giving me something more to think about than just breasts and what on earth was happening with her body. If only I was able to turn back the clock, would I have been able to prevent any of this from happening? I just didn't have the answer because it had crept up on us swiftly, silently and with devastating consequences. There wasn't a definitive starting point when I could say that that was when it all started. Yesterday, she was a carefree girl, swimming, dancing, running laughing and in a heartbeat, she was replaced with a woman's body that weighed her down, making her feel awkward, dirty and guilty, none of which was due to something she had done but due to what she had become.

Unfortunately, for me to be able to relax was difficult. I was so saddened, shocked and truly incredulous that this had all happened within the last six months. How and why my daughter? Was it something I/we had done? Questions, questions, all of them repeating and going around in my head. I kept thinking about the appointment we had, as soon as were back from holiday. I was pinning my hopes on this but at the same time, I was very concerned as to the whys and wherefores of what was happening to her. I knew I had to appear emotionally composed on the outside; my insides, however, were churning away with worry. Just because we had this appointment, it certainly didn't mean that her big problem would automatically go away. Deep down, I knew we were, I was sorry to say, in it for the long haul.

5

The Very First Paediatric Consultation

"And I try, oh my God do I try
I try all the time, in this institution."

Diary extract, August 28th, 2007:

Searching for some answers to the question of, why has my daughter grown so big. Hoping upon hope that this first hospital appointment will provide us with some answers, some support, understanding and a way forward. We are a little desperate.

"I so, so hope, Mum, that when we go in, they'll be able to do something about it."

"Oh, I'm sure we will get some answers. Let's keep positive and believe that something will be done," I said with my fingers and everything else crossed.

I looked over at her dad, who was listening but not contributing, always the pragmatic member of our family, dealing with things sensibly and realistically. Don't let emotions cloud your judgement.

During the drive back from our holiday in France, my mind had been full of a hundred unanswered questions. Although we all appeared to have had a good holiday, it hadn't been without its difficulties. I was continually plagued with anxiety and nerves as to what this appointment would reveal. At the same time, I was desperately wanting it to reveal something and provide us with some answers that would help. Life was becoming too difficult for her and we needed something positive to cling onto.

At this time, we knew absolutely nothing about what was happening to her little body. All we knew was that both her breasts were growing at an alarming rate and that every month meant another increase in size. The sheer pace and speed of her growth were overwhelming. I felt that to consider it as simply puberty taking its course was absolute nonsense. I was determined not to allow anybody in the medical world to hoodwink me into thinking that hers was a normal size, if not a little on the outer spectrum. I also had resigned myself to the fact that there was only one way of getting rid of these shocking-sized breasts, other than a miracle. A breast reduction wasn't a pleasant realisation but what else could be done to remove these continually growing monsters?

So here we were at the hospital eager to be seen and even keener to be given some answers. Although straight away our little bit of hope was dented. The female paediatric consultant we'd explicitly requested wasn't available and my daughter was going to be seen by her male registrar. This was frustrating and disappointing. I felt the situation required some female empathy; somebody with their own pair of breasts at least. I had to wonder whether anyone had bothered to find out the reason for our appointment. I surely would have thought that as it was a young girl, with an unusual increase in breast growth, someone might have suggested that she was seen by another female Consultant, particularly as we had initially requested this. Isn't there any communication, liaison or connection within the system to ensure a patient is seen by the most appropriate professional? Urgh, deep breath and count to ten.

However, it was not to be, and we were called in from the waiting room by a small, late-thirties man, who if I'm honest wasn't somebody I wanted looking at my daughter's breasts. If I continue to describe him in more detail, there is no doubt, I would be considered biased and totally non-pc. The fact was that regardless of colour and creed, I simply didn't feel comfortable with any man looking quite so keenly at her. Whether this was wrong of me or not, it was how I felt.

"Good morning to you all. So, you're here because you think your daughter has early puberty, which we sometimes call precocious puberty."

Precocious puberty is when a child's body begins changing into that of an adult too soon, before age eight in girls. He looked over at her as he said this and whether or not he was expecting a reply from her, I don't know. Did she know what it was? No, of course, she didn't. At 12 years old all she knew was that life had dealt her a very tricky and disabling card. I took a deep breath, swallowed hard, made a quick decision not to say anything about the distinct lack of female medical attention and said,

"Well, um, possibly that may be true but what she is dealing with at the moment and why we are here to see you is because of her rapid increase in breast growth and we have no idea why this is happening and if and when it will stop."

"Are there family members who have large breasts? It may be possible that she has inherited this and that her growth will stabilise and stop?"

"No, no there is no one and as you can see, she has a tiny frame and I really do feel that as she is only 12, her breast size is simply far too big."

"Well let's examine her and see. It might also be that she is on the outer edge of the growth spectrum."

Here we go, no, that's not right I thought, how bloody irritating. I will not allow him to believe this or trick me into believing it. It was impossible to comprehend that her size was normal. It just couldn't be right. It really matters how medical professionals choose their words, it can change the way a patient and her family feel, and he'd chosen his words poorly.

She rather reluctantly but dutifully removed her top and lay down on the examination couch. As the registrar examined her, he was visibly concerned. I'm assuming his concern was about the size, and how hot they were to the touch, but he didn't say as much. He appeared to be at a loss.

"If you don't mind, I think I will ask a colleague to take a look and give his opinion," he said. A rhetorical question probably but I did mind, not that it made any difference.

We were crushed, not only did he appear to be clueless, but he invited in yet another male medical colleague. This was, I suppose, something that we were all going to have to accept. So, my daughter lay there exposed for the second time to another stranger while he struggled to find something medically worthwhile to say. I did think, once again, how much easier it may have been for my daughter and us if a female consultant had been present.

I can honestly say that throughout Ellen's long and difficult journey, the medical professionals she saw were predominantly male. I am not sexist and I'm certainly not a man-hater, but I do believe this fact had a bearing on how the disease was perceived and on how, in some cases, she was treated. It begs the question, what if a little boy had come in with grossly enlarged testicles, that were six times their normal size, would he have received more empathy and understanding? Would appointments have been swifter and more informative? Any shred of modesty she had disappeared with this disease and she found herself on display to an assortment of medical professionals every step of the way. The top part of her body simply became an object which was discussed, felt, prodded, poked, stared and wondered at, with very little results in return; emotionally and physically demanding for any adult let alone a young prepubescent girl.

The outcome of their discussion, even with a second opinion, was disappointingly vague. Even though the registrar, whom I had decided to nickname Dr I Know Nothing, for obvious reasons, had appeared shocked by her size, I had a suspicious feeling that his underlying impression was that she was simply on the outer edge of the growth spectrum. Way off the scale, I would suggest. I described how her size was seriously impeding her life but surely, he could have seen this for himself? It didn't take much intelligence to realise how difficult her life had become trying to carry these huge breasts around with her. I asked where we should go from here, and tentatively brought up the possibility of a breast reduction. He seemed to baulk at this and insisted it was too early to say; more tests were needed and, finally, that she was too young.

This made me laugh. Too young indeed. She was most certainly TOO YOUNG, at the age of twelve, for size E-cup bras. The appointment ended with Dr I Know Nothing promising to discuss the case with his colleagues in London. And what, pray, was she to do in the meantime? I couldn't help but imagine the size she'd be when a diagnosis was finally made, but it wasn't something I wanted to think about. God only knew what her fate would be. As a result, we were, still, totally in the dark as to what was happening to her.

This lack, seemingly, of any immediate action and the thought of the size she would be when a decision as to how the problem should be dealt with had been made, was a truly bitter blow. He did, however, mention the name of a Plastic Surgeon Consultant who he thought might be able to help. I pressed him for the details, thinking this was better than nothing. I felt we had to come away from this appointment with information that may help my daughter's case. A name of a consultant who could help us was crucial in keeping our hopes up.

I suppose I had to be fair, as a family, we had become accustomed to her size and the associated difficulties. Dr I Know Nothing, on the other hand, wasn't really up to speed with it all and so his comments about being too early to discuss a breast reduction, were fair enough, I think. He did say that we were to make another appointment with him in six weeks. Oh, me, oh my, he really hadn't considered, or maybe he just hadn't listened, or most probably hadn't believed a rather distressed mother, when I explained to him about her body's incredible and devastating ability to grow. The thought of how big she would be by then was truly frightening. I began to wonder if there was anyone out there that could make them go away, or at least stop them from growing. The answer at this time was quite simply, no. The information we had been given was paltry, to say the least, and that was all we had.

We left this appointment feeling very deflated and dejected and wondered whether making another visit to see Dr I Know Nothing was going to be of any use. In fact, to be absolutely honest, all three of us felt his attitude and approach to my daughter as a patient and to the problem itself was pretty lacking in professionalism. Instead of giving us even a minuscule amount of hope and understanding, we walked out of his consultation room feeling worse than we did before we went in.

I had been unable to find any information or examples of children this young, who had grown breasts the size she was at this time. Yet, it was unthinkable that she was the only one in the whole world who was struggling with this insidious disease which was corrupting her small body. I certainly didn't wish what was happening to my daughter on anybody, but I so wanted there to be somebody that knew and had experienced what we were going through. It would have made life far more palatable and her circumstances easier to deal with, if she, we, hadn't felt alone with this problem. We needed to have some sort of an idea as to where to go from here and where it would ultimately lead her.

To make matters worse, the follow-up appointment with Dr I Know Nothing, was postponed by a further three weeks. I was furious, wasn't anyone taking this seriously? I rang to complain and vent my feelings, how could they possibly expect her to wait almost another month? Did they not even think about the size she would be by then? Apparently not. The result of my rantings was to bring the appointment forward by a week. Oh yippee, that's helpful.

We did return for the follow-up appointment, which was at the end of September, but it was no better than the first and although she underwent many tests, we just didn't think that he took ownership of her problem. For Dr I Know Nothing, she was obviously not a typical patient, he clearly didn't know how to deal with her problem and perhaps, it was easier for him to consider that we were parents who were overreacting.

It was at this point that I decided to take matters into my own hands. A realisation that however good the NHS is, (and it is), the speed at which you get answers and appointments is limited to a snail's pace. I suppose the volume of patients in the NHS contributes to these delays. What's the saying, 'The Mill of God grinds slowly', well it certainly applied to the NHS. I resolutely wouldn't give up and was determined that time played an enormous factor in the well-being of my daughter. We couldn't just sit around waiting whilst all the time her body was a ticking time bomb, any larger and who knows what would happen.

I contacted our doctor and requested a referral to another paediatric consultant. This time I decided against requesting a female consultant. I'd learnt my lesson last time. We were prepared to see him privately and if it meant going to London and paying money, so be it. We had also made an initial, private appointment to see the plastic surgeon recommended on our first visit to Dr I Know Nothing. This was to be in October and how she would be, both mentally and physically by then we just did not have any idea. I wasn't sure how much examining my daughter could take but unfortunately, she had no choice. We were, quite honestly, just happy that we had these appointments. As long as it appeared that her situation was being looked at and hopefully dealt with, I felt positive, but doing nothing was tantamount to giving up and leaving it all up to the slow workings of the medical world, which I refused to do.

It came down to this simple equation; not having appointments meant not being any further forward with resolving the situation and not being able to solve the problem meant more unhappy days ahead for my daughter. All the time her body was left to its own devices, the situation would worsen. Appointments were fundamental in order to progress, no matter how great or small, they were the key.

6

First Cosmetic Surgery Consultation

Diary extract, 15th October 2007:

She's struggling with an H-cup, well quite frankly, who wouldn't be? We're still looking for answers. Maybe even a name for whatever it is she has got, although gigantic breasts seemed to fit pretty well. Dr I Know Nothing was of no help at all, except to give us the name of the consultant we are seeing today. A great deal is riding on this appointment.

By the time this appointment had arrived, her breasts had grown to a size H and to put it into real terms, a honeydew melon would be a good example.

I considered it crucial to try and get the ball rolling and manipulate the system. By this I mean making private appointments, harassing the NHS and private consultants, by phone, by letter and generally making a nuisance of myself. All this to prevent time from ticking away and with each tick the worry of increased growth. Left to my own devices, all I could do was worry. This particular appointment was made privately with the Plastic Surgeon Consultant, who Dr I Know Nothing had recommended back in August. We felt that by paying for an appointment, we would get at least thirty minutes of consultation time with someone who may know more and would listen to what we had to say. In effect, we were paying for a little peace of mind.

As we arrived at the entrance to the drive, the impressive red brick, listed building, dating back to the 1800s, loomed in front of us. We found ourselves in the most beautiful grounds, with views of the sea, and a building which was once a boarding school. The immediate effect was one of peace and calm, giving me a sense of optimism that we may find ourselves a bit further forward than we had been since August. I hoped that this meeting would be a different experience and a far cry from our first meeting with Dr I Know Nothing, where parking had been impossible and the building was a mass of corridors with signs that misled rather than helped. Added to that, a professional who provided us with no real information and who didn't make any effort to ease the situation that Ellen was in by offering a few reassuring words.

We were shown into the consultation room and greeted by a charming and friendly man, who welcomed us with a smile and whom we all immediately liked. This Consultant sitting opposite us oozed efficiency and most of all looked concerned and genuinely meant it. To quote my daughter:

He didn't creep me out, like some of the other men. I found him really reassuring even though I knew I wasn't saying a great deal. He was patient and more consoling than consulting."

What could I say to that? Except perhaps to wonder why there couldn't be more consultants like him. A little bit of kindness, a smile and showing you care, goes a long way. It costs nothing and takes up very little time but meant so much to this young patient. I wistfully thought that perhaps in another life I would come back as the most caring, attentive, sympathetic, understanding, emotionally and professionally intuitive female paediatric consultant of all time. I would be a highly sought-after, intelligent medical professional who had reached the pinnacle of her career. Ah well, for the time being, it was back in the room.

My daughter remembers him gently lifting her breasts and looking very pensive and thoughtful, explaining that because of their weight the skin was very stretched. He highlighted the enormity of the issue and the vast amount of breast tissue that she was struggling to carry around with her. As he carefully examined her, what was so good to see was that she visibly relaxed with him and felt confident in his care. He was extremely understanding and his diagnosis was that she was a young girl with a slim frame, a BMI (body mass index) of 19.5, with Gigantomastia (large heavy breasts – Grade III ptosis). In layman's terms, she was a little girl who now wore size H-cup bras, with severe sagging of the breasts in which the nipple lay well below the place where the breast and the chest meet. She also suffered from back and neck pain and soreness under the breasts, and the cause of this trauma was idiopathic (no known cause). These were just a few of the physical problems she had to deal with, on a daily basis.

Completing his examination, he sat back down behind his desk, asking her to get dressed and join in with the conversation. Both my husband and I sat anxiously waiting. He finally said how pretty, sensible and mature she was. Well, that was enough to send us both into floods of tears, adding that he sympathised with her predicament and thought she was an amazing young lady, especially in view of how her problem was affecting her life. He shuffled a box of tissues towards us which we all gladly accepted. Tears were now really flowing; up to then, there hadn't been anyone who was so kind, understanding and knowledgeable and offered us a way forward. I was in love; so far this appointment was everything we wanted it to be and was worth its weight in gold.

"What she is dealing with is a rare condition known as Juvenile Gigantomastia, which causes excessive growth of the female breasts. In your daughter's case, because she is so young, it is very rare. Gigantomastia can occur randomly but as well as occurring during puberty, it can also occur during pregnancy or after taking certain medications. It is considered a benign disease, but it can be physically disabling if not treated."

Well, ain't that the truth, I thought, nodding vigorously, sitting spellbound, clutching our tissues, trying to stem the tide of tears. This was what we wanted to know, yes, yes!

He continued to tell us that it can also be called breast

hypertrophy or macromastia both of which refer to a condition involving developing extremely large breasts due to excessive breast tissue growth. He cleared his throat, smiled and continued,

"The way forward is for a breast reduction. I could help you with surgery, but we need to think very carefully before proceeding with this course of action."

"Yes, we completely understand," we said in unison and with a slow exhale of breath. We had been given some answers and a name, this was a major step forward. At last.

He went into further detail, saying that there was a lot to do before a breast reduction could go ahead.

"More information from the various investigations that you have had needs to be obtained, as it is important to exclude any underlying problems before committing to surgery."

"Yes, that is absolutely reasonable." We wholeheartedly agreed, almost delirious from the information we had received, but not ready to hear what came next.

"You must also be aware that this is an extremely uncommon problem," he continued. "As your daughter is very young, you need to know that there is a chance of further breast development after surgery. If this is the case, it may result in her having to undergo a double mastectomy."

Bam! Just like that.

Suddenly, it was as though all the air had been sucked out of the room. A double mastectomy, had we heard correctly? Oh my God, the spell was well and truly broken. That can't be right. I was freefalling from a great height. Answers, yes, we wanted answers but certainly not to get so much more than we bargained for, never, never this. We were stunned into silence; this was too shocking to comprehend. She's only twelve, you must have got it wrong. I coped by going into ostrich mode. Head firmly in the sand, I told myself that, although we all appreciate honesty, he was giving us the absolute worst-case scenario, it obviously wouldn't ever come to that. She would have the reduction, sail through the healing process and voila a pair of perfect breasts that were entirely appropriate for the twelve-year-old girl she was.

Through my shock, I managed to look over at my husband who was gravely struggling to put it into some kind of a practical box in his head. Neither of us could look at each other or our daughter. Did she understand what had just been said? She was so, so young, would she have understood? More than that, did I want to be the one to have to explain? Were there even words I could use that would be sufficient, sensitive and without too much emotion? Are there any books on the best way to tell your young daughter, who hasn't even gone through puberty, that she may have to have all her breasts lopped off?

It hadn't even occurred to us that her breasts would continue to grow after a reduction. This appointment, which had been going so very well, was now all shot to pieces. A big question mark had been stuck very rudely over the success of a breast reduction, shattering our hopes. How could we be so stupid and naive to think that a reduction would solve the problem? I reluctantly had to accept that just as there was no explanation for the growth, nor was there any reason to expect she would stop growing after a reduction. It wasn't as if her body would be dictated to by the operation. Whatever was causing this growth was probably not going to be deterred by the removal of tissue.

We sat, staring at him blankly, at this last earth-shattering bit of news, with a feeling of impending doom and a severe crushing of our spirit. What else could we do? What else was there to do? I reached, yet again, for the box of tissues but even my tears had dried up. I do believe he continued to talk to us but I had gone into my head.

Right, I thought. Get the crying over with, keep it together and forge some kind of path through this quagmire of information. It was vital to push the possibility of a double mastectomy aside and focus on what needed to be done now. He only said that it *may* happen and not that it would. We must, *must*, remember that fact. I had made an instant decision to say very little about what had been said and to concentrate on telling Ellen that a breast reduction was now looking much more likely. I didn't want a discussion, just yet, about what happened to her if her breasts continued to grow after a reduction, let's just take one step at a time.

There were, however, things to do, so I couldn't remain stunned and mute for long. As he had explained, before surgery could take place, it was important for him to obtain all the results from the tests that she had so far undergone. I wasn't sure exactly which tests these were. Trying to focus on tests rather than a mastectomy, I had to suppose they were the ones that had been done at the same time as the second consultation with Dr I Know Nothing, at the end of September. Honestly, am I expected to know this? I thought to myself. Apparently so. Fine, ok, no problem I was on it.

Feeling totally despondent, I did wonder whether it mattered what tests they were because it didn't detract from the fact that she was in desperate need of a breast reduction, with or without these tests. However, test results are important and if it's test results he wants, its test results he'll get. As usual, time was of the essence because the little we did know about this disease was that it waited for no man, least of all consultants and surgeons and the NHS. Every hour, day, or week that went by meant another centimetre or two was added to her size. I felt that it made sense to assume that the bigger the breasts, the more difficult the operation.

As well as the importance of acquiring test results, which had sent me into yet another frenzy of telephone calls and letter writing, she also had to be seen by the hospital's paediatric arts psychotherapist due to her young age. This was necessary before any sort of breast surgery could take place and was one of the criteria set by the plastic surgeon, who I had now nicknamed Mr Charmingly-Direct. Art therapy is a form of psychotherapy that uses art media as its main mode of expression and communication to address confusing and distressing emotional issues. I agreed that this was extremely important, not least because it gave her a chance to vent her feelings and talk to someone who wasn't personally involved. As parents, we supported, talked and argued our way through the problem but ultimately, we were personally involved and had our own issues to deal with. So, while it meant yet another appointment, weekly visits were arranged.

"I didn't really say too much, during these sessions, it was difficult to know how I really felt, and I just didn't know what to say sometimes. The therapist was very gentle, and patient and I was happy to have these visits."

It mustn't be underestimated that she had been cheated of the normal age-appropriate enjoyment of her developing body. She was never able to join in any 'girlie' conversations about buying bras, as this had been so traumatic for her, or indeed finding any clothes that fitted properly. I also never had the opportunity to enjoy gradually seeing my daughter develop physically. Instead, she went from her sweet A-cup to H-cup in just eight months and understandably, I had a growing sense of shock, horror and overwhelming helplessness, wondering how, where and when this was all going to end.

Appointments, as you can see, were crucial, even if this last appointment had given us more than we had anticipated. They were the key to moving her problem forward and with one very informative private appointment under our belts, we had two more planned. This time one in London during the day and a second meeting, in the evening with this same charming Consultant, Mr Charmingly-Direct, in the beautiful building by the sea. Busy, busy, busy!

The disadvantage of having two appointments in one day was the question of how much examining my daughter could take in one day. It was unanswerable.

7

You Cannot Be Serious!

"I realised quickly when I knew I should
That the world was made up of this brotherhood of man
For whatever that means."

Diary extract, 19th November 2007:

Today is a huge ask for her, we have two private appointments to attend: an appointment in the morning in London to get a second opinion on what exactly is going on and another one much later in the day, to find out what can be done when we're returning to see Mr Charmingly-Direct, who has an attractive and kind manner but he does say it how it is; I suppose I get why he does. Ellen, however, is currently struggling with a size K/ L, increased to the size of a rather large watermelon now. To be honest, after discovering last month from Mr Charmingly-Direct what the worst scenario could be, I do feel as if I'm hovering on the brink, hopefully, not a disastrous one.
Only time will tell.

We were up with the larks; the boys were complaining about having to go to school whilst we were having a day trip to London; not quite! I thought it futile to explain that the circumstances surrounding this trip made it the opposite of fun and that a normal school day would probably be a better option; they wouldn't have believed me. Once we had dropped them off at 0800 outside school, with bags and PE kit in tow, we headed straight to London to make the 1030 appointment.

Driving to London meant having to take into consideration the traffic and also, having been told by the hospital that parking in the area was limited, ensuring we could park the car and still make it to the appointment without rushing. As neither of us had been to this hospital before it was important to allow plenty of time. What we didn't want was to be rushed and arrive out of breath, keeping the Consultant waiting by being late.

The journey went very smoothly; we arrived with half an hour to spare, found a private car park, handed over the keys as requested, in case they needed to move the car and headed for the hospital. We let the receptionist know we were there and then sat down feeling very glad that we had made it with time to spare. We chatted, looked at the magazines and waited and waited and waited and waited some more. None of us wanted to acknowledge the fact to each other that we had been sitting in the waiting room for far too long, not wanting to add to our already overloaded stress levels.

At one point, I went to check that we had been given the right time; maybe we had got it wrong? But the receptionist just smiled and said that it shouldn't be much longer. Finally, after waiting fifty-five minutes, she asked me over to the desk to take a call from the Consultant. That's strange; surely, he should be here in his office not on the other end of the telephone? This was unexpected and I had the feeling that it wasn't going to be good news, certainly not in our favour. My conversation with him went a bit like this:

"Ok, so, let me get this straight, you have a problem with your boiler at home, so how does that leave us and when do you think you'll get here, or at least how close to London do you live?"

"You live in the outskirts of Surrey, ah right, (pause, deep breath), so probably not for several hours then?"

"Oh, just after lunch time. It's 1130 now, so I suppose we'll see you at whatever time you manage to get here?"

"No, don't bother ringing my mobile, I'll give you my husband's, you can ring him," I seethed between gritted teeth.

So much for being on the brink and overloaded stress levels, at that moment I felt I was going right over the edge, my heart was racing with the sudden increase in adrenaline brought about by this very inconsiderate man, whom I never wanted to speak to again. My husband could take the strain and speak with him about whatever time he decided to pitch up. I did not want to have anything more to do with his boiler problem. What sort of a person was he? Such a poor excuse. He surely couldn't be serious. He had, quite literally, verbally insulted all three of us. Trying to stay calm was not an option but as always, I had to.

I vaguely remember trying to compose myself and organise my thoughts, for Ellen's sake more than anything else. She needed as much positivity as she could get at this moment in her life and I was damned if I'd let this Consultant derail her. Two pairs of eyes were focussed on me as I headed over to where we had all been sitting for the last hour and plonked myself down.

"Well, what an interesting conversation," I said, raising my eyes skyward and taking a deep breath. "It would seem that the good consultant has had a crisis, a few technical problems at home, namely his boiler and because of this, he won't be with us until this afternoon."

They both looked at me. My daughter knew this wasn't good, which made me feel even worse and my husband sat there his face saying it all, knowing that I was about to lose it.

"Unbelievable!" I continued. "He won't be with us for quite a while because of his broken boiler! You would have thought it would have been more prudent and professional if he, Mr Boilerman, (I quickly decided to aptly give him this nickname), had lied and told me the reason for his delay was a meeting or something similar, rather than his boiler," Pausing for breath, I continued, "And, have you noticed." I said looking around the room, "That all the time we've been sitting here there have been few patients if any waiting with us. Don't you think that's strange?" This fact had just occurred to me and in a state of heightened emotion, I started to laugh suggesting that it was some kind of conspiracy or even somebody from 'You've been

Framed' was going to jump out on us. They both looked at me failing to see the funny side of this situation.

Ignoring my comments, my husband said decisively, "Right, let's get out of here, get some fresh air and find somewhere to eat, that will kill a few hours."

Good plan I thought and as we walked out, feeling unbelievably let down, I looked over at the receptionist and threw her a few dirty looks, no doubt she had been in on this duplicity from the outset. How could she!

What Mr Boilerman didn't realise because it was obviously of little importance to him, was how important this appointment was to us, to keep our morale lifted, to feel action was being taken, even if it was only small steps towards the all-important outcome. Not only that, did he realise all the trouble we had gone to in order to see him.? This was serious organisation and the Consultant had the gall to tell me he wouldn't make it on time because he had a god damn boiler problem at home. Yeah well, my daughter has a much bigger problem, two in fact, sort that one out! Oh but, how can you? You're not here.

Even now, after many years have gone by, when I think of this moment, I still find myself shaking my head incredulously and wondering what really was going on. Did he at any point have misgivings for admitting to us that he had this nasty little problem which had extended our waiting time by not just minutes, not hours but by half a day? If the truth be told it wasn't the wait so much as the thought that he obviously didn't really understand, sympathise or appreciate the enormous difficulties my daughter was going through. As a result of Mr Boilerman's domestic problems, it was necessary to extend the time for the car park and as parking was limited around the hospital, we didn't want to have to move it again. My husband went to sort this out and we waited, we were getting good at this. He returned quite a while later, looking, how we all felt, confused, perplexed and downright angry. This was a private car park with attendants and the car had been moved, which shouldn't have been a problem, except they informed my husband that the wing mirror was broken, and did we know? Ooh now, let me think, no, no, funnily enough, we didn't know because, guess what, both mirrors were intact when we left it earlier on in the morning.

There were three witnesses to this crime, yer honour, to confirm that the wing mirror was absolutely, undeniably properly attached to the car before we brought it and left it on these premises. That could only mean that the damage was carried out sometime between the hours of 1015 and 1145. We had proof that none of us were anywhere near the car at that time. I rest my case and want to be properly reimbursed! The car parking manager, or whoever he was, did not want to admit to the damage but as all three of us were so fired up, he eventually backed down and we paid nothing. Too right. This day and it was only just gone midday, was becoming a truly spectacular disaster.

The particular area of London where the hospital was situated, to put it bluntly, and in my humble opinion, which to be fair was by now extremely tainted, is not a place I would return to in a hurry. We took refuge in a well-known, cheap and cheerful restaurant and whiled away two hours eating, drinking and trying to keep our spirits up. My husband played let's find the coins that had fallen out of customers' pockets and become lodged down the backs of chairs. It was distracting if nothing else, and I think he won, having found a grand total of £2.

Meanwhile, as they were both busy, I was allowing myself to wallow in disbelief and self-pity. How could Mr Boilerman have such little regard for us, for Ellen and put his boiler first, before an appointment that was so important to the patient? I was wracking my brain, trying to come to a rational reason as to why. This being only our second-ever private medical appointment, it did cross my mind that, maybe, this sort of thing happens, and it wasn't anything out of the ordinary. It seemed a little odd though and also terribly unprofessional. It certainly wasn't anything like our fabulous visit to Mr Charmingly-Direct, who was based in such lovely surroundings and didn't appear to have any domestic problems. Maybe he just didn't have a boiler?

My mobile rang and to my absolute, unequivocal surprise, the call was from the previous Paediatric Registrar, Dr I know Nothing, who we had seen in August and then again in September in our local hospital. You may remember that we had a fairly low opinion of him, and my impression then was that he came across as being fairly dismissive of Ellen's problem. His follow-up appointment was postponed and pushed back to a later appointment, and I complained about not only the delay but also that he had not passed on the results of her tests which had been taken. Believe me, I had stressed to all and sundry that these tests were of the utmost importance; this delay meant that the possibility of surgery was still only just a distant wish.

However, amazingly enough, his call was to tell me that the results had been forwarded to the appropriate departments. I have to say I was taken aback, agreeably so, by what I had just heard. This was super, good news indeed and quite interesting timing.

From October onwards, I decided to make a complaint against Dr I Know Nothing because, as I saw it, there was a lack of any help or action and promised results. In truth, however, I didn't have the energy or time to follow this through. My supposition and it is only that, albeit based on the facts as I saw them, was that consultants tend to stick together. I'm not sure what the collective noun for consultants is if there is one. I vaguely wondered if the cause of our delay was a result of my complaints about Dr I Know Nothing having perhaps, filtered down to Mr Boilerman, who we were supposed to be seeing today. Interestingly, and I mean very interestingly, immediately after my call, my husband received the call from Mr Boilerman, saying he would be there at 2.30, our original appointment was for 1030. Well, well, well, Watson, what do you make of that?

So, let's do a bit of detective work, was this coincidence or was there a connection between the two calls? Hercule Poirot, Sherlock Holmes, Miss Marple, Columbo any ideas? Whatever the reason, now was not the time to ponder over the clues. So, we put our best foot forward and made our way back to the hospital and back to the reception area to see Mr Boilerman. It did cross my mind that I must remember to use his correct name. Gosh, I wasn't sure I knew it.

Finally, finally, finally, after receiving his call that we were now to have the pleasure of seeing him, we were shown into his office, which was a very basic room with several chairs and what looked like an examination couch. He was a tall, round-faced, almost cherubic-looking man. Nothing like the two-headed monster with fangs and claws, which I had vividly conjured up in my mind. He laughed off his problem with the boiler and briefly deigned to apologise for his lateness. I was, to say the least, furious and alright I didn't expect him to get down on his knees and beg our forgiveness, I did expect a little more of an apology than that. I don't consider myself to be vindictive, but I fervently wished that as we spoke, his boiler had exploded and water was spewing out all over his house. Oh yes, that thought, at least, managed to put a smile on my face and slightly cheered me up.

Quelle surprise! All he could tell us was a repeat of what we had already been told; my daughter's rapid growth of breast tissue was idiopathic, no known cause. We were there for less than ten minutes when he asked, with finality, if we had any further questions. Now, don't get me wrong, the last thing I wanted was for Ellen to be continually on show, to whoever we were seeing at the time, however, I was forced into asking him,

"Umm, don't you think it is important to have a look at her breasts? As well as the increase in size, which seems to be continuing, she has now developed sores underneath the area where they rub her skin?"

This, to me, seemed a fairly reasonable request, not least if you considered the length of time we had waited, the cost of the appointment and how little of his time he had given to us. I did wonder whether this was yet another anomaly of making a private appointment; examinations are extra?

I stared fixedly at him as I spat out these words, requesting an examination, which was simple enough and, come on, I was being very polite. He had to be joking; didn't he have any intention of taking a medical stance by examining her? His reaction was more than a little strange and I was sure that this two-headed monster was going to rear both of his ugly heads and proceed to bite my head off. All I can suppose is that as she was wearing a thick jacket, and we all know that clothes can hide a multitude of sins, he must have thought we were being overly worried parents and her growth, heaven help us, was normal. We, however, not surprisingly wanted, actually no, bloody well expected, to be taken seriously. Why would we have made this appointment otherwise? It beggared belief.

I just couldn't think of any reason why you wouldn't examine a patient. Surely an examination is the only way to assess the problem? It's also worth pointing out, that by the beginning of November she was now a size K-cup, oh yes indeed! This was not a size to be reckoned with, least of all by a girl of twelve. My poor daughter knew how angry I was feeling and just kept looking between me and Mr Boilerman, knowing that it was, sadly, all about her. He acquiesced and asked her to remove her jacket and top and to jump up onto the examining coach.

Jump up! Jump up! Thoughtless, stupid man, didn't he know that she was physically incapable of jumping anywhere? She hadn't been able to jump, run, leap or any other normal activity that any young girl should be able to do, for a long time. For the second or third time during this whole debacle, I thought about how important it was for the medical world to choose its words wisely, for goodness' sake. Silly me, I thought, doing an imaginary slapping of my forehead, of course, he hadn't taken this into consideration because his thoughts had been on his boiler and not on my daughter's problem. He had been applying his superior brain to the workings, or not, of his central heating system.

So, she clambered wearily onto the bed, removed her jacket and jumper and then with my help, whilst I threw daggers at this idiot of a man, she removed her size K bra. Poor girl.

Bingo!

Top half off and his expression changed radically; they were huge and the sores where they rubbed were weeping. He actually began to take us seriously and his actions spoke volumes. Within the next five minutes we were being seen by a Senior Breast Surgeon who was kind, seemingly understanding of her situation, if not of her disease, and showed her some care. There is a God, after all, that's all we wanted, private appointment or not.

She was whisked down to his clinic and was given an ultrasound scan of her breasts to exclude any 'pathology other than idiopathic hypertrophy/ hyperplasia', which means ruling out any other reason, other than the no known cause, that may have contributed to her excessive growth. We had, at last, been taken seriously and with consideration; this was vindication and almost worth the wait and the wing mirror.

She was examined, she was x-rayed and she had a variety of other tests, including her first biopsy, which wasn't great.

"They will numb the area first, so don't worry, you won't feel anything," I said encouragingly. Fine for me to say. I wasn't the one lying there with my arm up and breasts on display.

"How big is the needle?"

"I'm not sure but it's important that a sample of your tissue is taken, this is a step further towards getting the operation, it's definitely worth it," I countered as I sat with her and watched this rather large needle inserted into her very large breast and not for the first time or the last, I fervently wished I could swap places with her.

"All done, you're very brave, you can get dressed now and the feeling in your breast will come back shortly." This very kind doctor gave her a quick squeeze of her arm and with a smile, he disappeared, and my daughter was dressed and ready to leave.

"Have you seen the time? We are going to have to get a move on," I said as we raced out of the hospital.

"We can only drive so fast." Forever practical, my husband.

Time was ticking as we rushed to the car and on to our next

appointment, which was the second cosmetic surgery consultation, with Mr Charmingly-Direct, and was a good ninety miles from where we were. We had no option but to drive straight from this appointment to the next. I had to make frantic phone calls to the Grandparents to ask them to stay on until we got back, which probably wouldn't be until around 9.30 pm. Emotions were running very high, and fatigue was setting in. I glanced to the back of the car and my daughter looked completely worn out and drained of any colour; what had we done to her? Food was the answer, or at least that was all I could provide to console her, so I rummaged in my bag and handed her something to munch on.

We left this appointment at 4.30 in the afternoon; it was already dark and the traffic at that time in London starts to build up. It wasn't a pleasant journey to the next appointment, but we knew that the tests had been sent, and more tests had been taken and this at least made us feel that the ball was well and truly rolling.

Before I move on, it is just worth mentioning that we were never charged for this private appointment, the fee was waived. More questions for those investigating sleuths. The question is why? Why indeed? I can only surmise: maybe it was because we were right about our daughter needing some expert help and he was wrong in thinking otherwise; maybe he felt guilty about our long wait; maybe he just felt sorry for my daughter or perhaps he had heard about our wing mirror? Whatever the reason, we will probably never find out but an interesting conundrum to ponder over.

8

Same Day and Second Cosmetic Consultation

Mr Boilerman was now a good ninety miles away and amazingly we had arrived on time for this second consultation having, I'm sure, broken more than a few traffic regulations. It was no mean feat driving like maniacs from the Capital to the South Coast in an hour and a half as if our lives depended on it. However, here we were once again back in this very pleasant building with its picturesque grounds. Even though darkness prevented us from seeing them, simply knowing they were there made all the difference. We were the only ones in the waiting room and the entire building was still and calm, a far cry from the hustle and bustle earlier in the day.

We were all completely spent, physically and mentally, especially Ellen. She had been put through some unpleasant experiences, not helped by the long delay and more than likely still had further investigations to undergo. More undressing, more poking and prodding and more debating. Such was Ellen's life at this time. The steaming cup of hot chocolate she'd been given on arrival went a long way to perking her up and after the second cup, she was more upbeat. In we went, "Once more unto the breach dear friends." I hoped that with one battle down we were not going to be embarking on another.

Mr Charmingly Direct greeted us with his usual air of calm authority.

"Nice to see you all again. So, I've received all the test results today and they were all normal which is reassuring."

We sat like expectant lapdogs, waiting for the next morsel

he'd throw our way. I was trying to gauge where that left us and wondering what he was going to say next, or how many hoops we may still have to jump through.

He gave a brief smile at which point my breath tightened. What did this smile mean? What were normal results? Normal wasn't part of our life just now. I was pretty sure I didn't even know what normal meant. He continued to explain that the ultra-scan showed no mass lesion. I wasn't quite sure exactly what this meant but I didn't want to interrupt him mid-flow. He continued,

"And the only logical way forward, therefore, is to go ahead and have the breast reduction," or as I thought, the bloody beast removed. A huge exhale of breath and I do believe we were all actually smiling. He carried on by saying, "I would like to see you at the NHS hospital in the next week or two and this will give you an opportunity to see the children's ward."

What relief, excellent news, which gave our spirits a much-needed lift. After getting off to such a horrible start that day, we could never have imagined it would end on such a high note. It was the best news and wiped out and obliterated the earlier events. There was finally some light at the end of the tunnel. We were giddy with euphoria, only a little tinged with exhaustion.

It is amazing how circumstances can alter; just when you think that life has got it in for you, it all changes and life becomes worth living again. These were Ellen's thoughts:

I was so very relieved after the awful day we had had, and I felt I could resign myself and let go as he actively took the reins. He saw the disaster for what it was. He was direct, professional and everything you'd expect from a medical 'professional'. I was very happy, and the hot chocolate was the cherry on top of a meeting, which was thankfully free of more looking and prodding.

At the end of this very long, rollercoaster of a day, we arrived back home and passed on the good news to the grandparents who had very kindly agreed to stay on and look after the boys. As much as our parents wanted to help and were concerned about their granddaughter, it was difficult for them to comprehend what was going on and why. They just knew we were so pleased with this outcome and if we were happy so were they. The boys were already in bed which meant they would have to wait until the morning before being given the news. Although, in reality their understanding of the importance of this operation was going to be limited. Why on earth would they be able to appreciate an operation like this one?

Feeling exhausted and on the verge of collapsing, Ellen fell into bed, knowing that there would be no school tomorrow. She deserved the luxury of having a day off, badly needing some downtime. Much to the boys' dismay, the next day, they were packed off to school and she stayed in bed. Life can be hard sometimes; something we were all too aware of. I began to behave as though the operation was a holiday, something to look forward to. Sure, our world had been turned upside down but where are the passports and tickets? What should we pack? How should we get there? Even when should I get my hair and nails done? It weirdly became something we were all looking forward to.

In the end, we had to wait another two and a half months for the surgery. Now it wasn't just my concern over size, more than anything I hated seeing my daughter struggle every day with the relentless and unstoppable growth of her chest. My heart was breaking for her, but I couldn't let her see. I felt we had to remain strong as a family and that my role as a mother was to demonstrate a will to fight. A small chink in my armour could quite easily become a void and we'd all get sucked in. We would deal with each day as it came and sooner or later things would be better.

Time v Size

My constant worry and again I didn't share this with Ellen, was that the size of her breasts, which were growing quickly, must surely influence the outcome of the operation. I understood that as intrusive and upsetting as they were, it was only right that my daughter underwent so many tests. It was vital to confirm that it was Juvenile Gigantomastia that was causing such rapid growth and nothing more nefarious. However, I was also all too aware that we were fighting against time. The operation needed to be done as soon as possible. I'm no expert, but it seemed logical to me that the more they grew, the more tissue would have to be removed and the more complicated the surgery would become. I had this strong belief that growing too big would be detrimental not just to her everyday physical and mental life but also when extracting so much tissue from her tiny, framed young body.

Before the operation, photographs of her breasts had to be taken at the hospital. Although she did her best, the photographer had a hard time containing her shock. The worst part of the ordeal was how distraught my daughter became. She was so ashamed of her body; she thought it ugly and grotesque. It was so painful to hear your twelve-year-old say these things about herself. I did my best to reassure her.

"Sweetheart, just let's look past them and think of how you will look after the operation."

"I don't want to think about it, I don't want to think about any of it. I just want them to go away."

She was beyond any kind of positive comments and encouragement. She desperately wanted to know why she was the only one on earth who had this problem. There just wasn't any answer; it was anybody's guess how many girls like Ellen have this - excuse the pun - huge burden. No matter how much we wanted to boost her morale and explain that it was all going to be alright, the fact was, no one knew for sure. All we could do in the end was to listen and accept what she was saying. The overriding wish for her was that this all-important operation would provide the positive outcome she was wanting, needing and most certainly deserved. There was nothing else in the world that I'd rather have, other than this not ever having happened at all.

Hospital photographs which may shock – taken in January 2008, aged twelve years, just before her breast reduction surgery in February 2008.

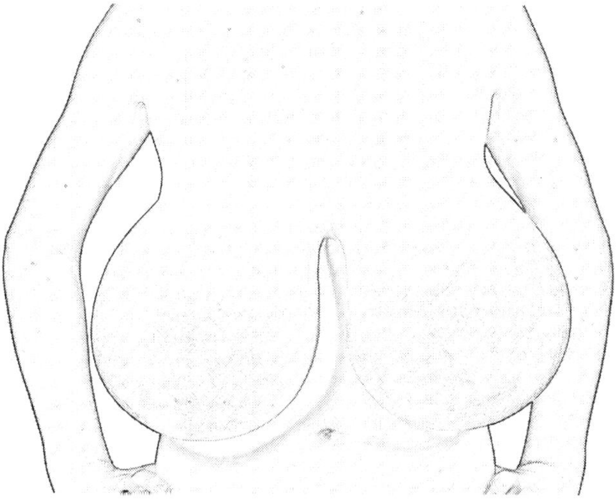

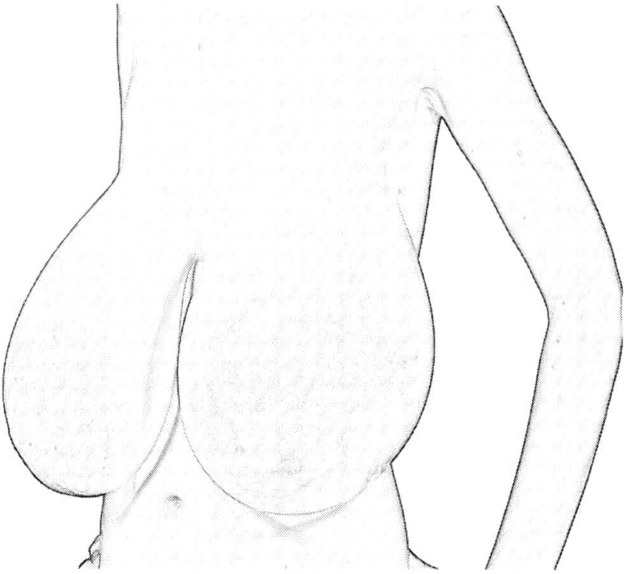

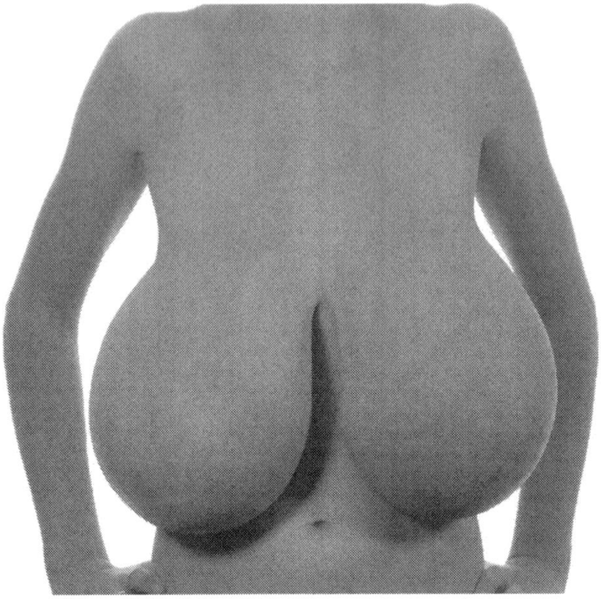

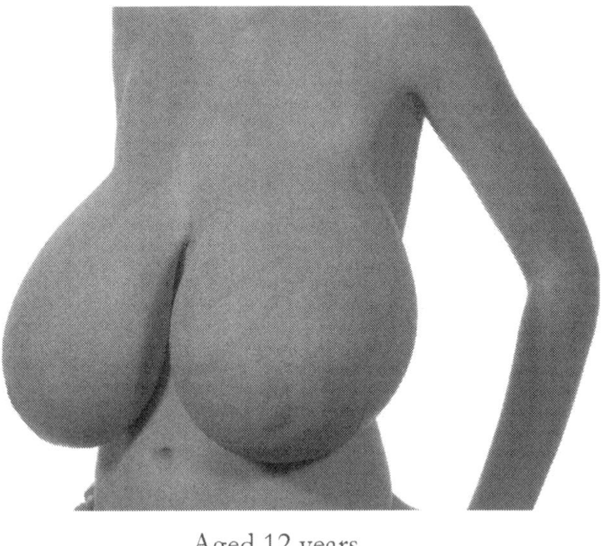

Aged 12 years.

9

The Great Reduction

A Bilateral breast reduction for Juvenile Gigantomastia

Diary extract, Friday 22nd February 2008:

It's early morning and I know there will be no time later to write this. What could be said about today – 'R', removal, reduction day, the much-needed and long-awaited big op. Finally! I wasn't sure, the nearer this date came, how I should or would be feeling; pleased because by the end of today she'd be rid of over half her breast size, yet so sad and worried about it happening and what if it doesn't go according to plan? Ellen's size was now an L and most definitely moving away from melons to pumpkins! It was essential for her to have this operation.
No doubt about it. Even so.

We had visited this specialist NHS hospital, Queen Victoria, many times before, leading up to this operation. It is a single-storey building which provides life-changing reconstructive surgery. It's functional and efficient, and who knew that behind this bland façade was a centre of excellence, world-famous for its pioneering burns and plastic surgery; she was in the right place. That said I don't think we would have cared if it was a cow shed in the middle of a field, we were so very glad to have arrived at this point.

I decided that I would stay with her in the hospital. When all was said and done, she was still my little girl, and this type of operation, it would seem, was only ever performed on adults. It was important for both of us that I was there 24 hours a day. I had been given a quick tour of my sleeping quarters when we had made the initial visit. It was a camp bed and had an adjacent shower and toilet cubicle; basic and functional and allowed me to always stay close to her.

The other decision we had made was that her dad had an opportunity to take the boys skiing. It was half-term and the dates coincided with the operation. It made sense for them to go, as there was nothing they could do and sitting at home wasn't going to help. It also meant that I could concentrate all my energy on her and not worry too much about the boys. I was relinquishing all responsibility knowing they were away and hopefully enjoying themselves. It made sense, even though I knew the decision to go wasn't taken lightly and their thoughts were with her.

Ellen was to share a ward with a 15-year-old girl who was there to have a breast augmentation. Her breasts were asymmetrical, and her operation was a corrective procedure to make both breasts the same and to look normal. Normal, there goes that word again, I had forgotten what that was by this point. Whether this was thoughtful planning by the NHS or not, I found it particularly helpful to be able to talk to the other girl's mother, even though the situation was only slightly similar. Ellen's reaction was a bit ambivalent; she didn't interact with the girl or show any interest. When I look back on these years, I believe she was suffering from shock; maybe this is an understatement. She was unable to fully comprehend what was happening to her body, how it had turned her world upside down and it would seem, was her problem alone.

"Well, here we are, it's really happening. A few weeks of convalescing and you'll be able to move forward." Once again, I was being cheerful but this time, I wholeheartedly believed in what I was saying. She was sitting on the hospital bed in the children's ward and gave me a rueful smile, whilst we waited for a visit from Mr Charmingly-Direct. Going under the knife isn't usually something that is looked forward to but her breast size was now an unmanageable L-cup and if it wasn't for the fact that I would put her life in danger and be thrown into prison I would have happily cut them off myself. To be able to see her first, rather than see her gigantic breasts - it's not called Gigantomastia for nothing - and to finally be relieved of this constant state of dread and despair was all I could hope for.

She changed into a hospital gown and we were led into a separate room where Mr Charmingly-Direct explained the procedure one more time. After examining her breasts, he then began to draw all over them. It was like a road map on two enormous mountains. And I can tell you, all I could think was how it represented our long uphill journey and one that would, hopefully, lead to us all being unburdened, and Ellen being unfettered and unchained, actually anything 'un' that stood in the way of her freedom. My fervent wish was that this would be a turning point leading to a normal life for her.

Unfortunately, I had this niggling memory and despite the hope and optimism, his words from October 2007 were playing on my mind,

"You must also be aware that this is an extremely rare problem and there is a chance of further breast development after surgery."

No, just shut up and keep quiet, I told myself. I would not allow this to creep into my thoughts, nor bury itself into my soul. Perhaps I was deluding myself, but I had to believe that everything that could be done was being done. All I could do now was think positively.

A breast reduction, on such a young girl and the size she was, wasn't something that happened too often in the children's ward, and I think we were the source of interest as well as sympathy. The nurses and all the consultants that she saw were all so supportive. It was encouraging and reminded me of what we'd been longing for, the removal of this abnormal growth. Even so, when they came to get her for the operation, I left the children's ward with her, feeling very sad and I could tell she was very nervous. She was drawn and quiet and we were both on the verge of tears. I squeezed her hand and kissed her forehead doing my best to reassure her it would all be over soon. I watched them give her the general anaesthetic, kissed her goodbye once more and walked back to the ward. Numb.

This, however, is what my daughter remembers:

I remember that the situation was super intense as I headed towards the theatre, with only a gown on, which didn't even properly do up at the back. I knew this was the right thing, but I was aware of not being able to hide myself anymore. For this operation to go ahead I had to undress and fully reveal what I was most ashamed of, to people who were Doctors. I was the most exposed I was ever going to be and had to really trust in them that they were going to improve my situation drastically - so there goes my gown – and most of my pride.

Having no way of determining the length of the operation, I was given a pager the size of what looked like a square brick, which would flash the moment I could go into the recovery room. It was a bit cumbersome and so for the first two hours, I remained close to the ward. After the third hour, feeling cabin feverish and agitated, I went for a walk just outside the hospital but still within the pager's reach. It had been raining and for an hour I surrendered myself to the elements, hoping that being outside would ease the awful, churning feeling inside and my constant thought that she was only twelve years old, still so young.

It began to rain heavily again so I decided enough was enough and went into one of several cafes within the hospital grounds. I plied myself with numerous cups of coffee and tried not to think about what was happening and what could go wrong. Quite by chance and very much to my surprise, I recognised one of the Registrars, who I knew was involved with her operation, buying himself a coffee. In a rather confused state, because I was sure it was him and yet couldn't understand why he was here, I stood up and walked over to him. It was impossible not to quiz him on how Ellen's operation was going. He was a little surprised to be confronted in the café, but he calmly explained that while one side of my daughter's chest had been completed, the other, put simply, wasn't behaving as it should. It had become necessary to rest the tissue for a while. This all sounded surreal and the more I tried to picture what he said the more distressing the situation seemed to be, but he was very kind and told me not to worry and that she was doing well. I suppose that was all he really could say, although I had visions of her being left on the operating table with half her chest completed and the other half being told to behave. It was best I didn't visualise this situation and just concentrate on coffee number four. Can days get any stranger?

Over half the day had disappeared and as I had come to know the area around the hospital very well, I anxiously returned to the parents' waiting room. Within five minutes I was released from my torment by the flashing of the brick.

Lying in her bed, looking very pale and wan, my daughter was taped and bandaged with a binder and had a tube on either side of her chest. She didn't look good but that was obviously to be expected. I held her hand, attempted a big smile and just sat with her, the absurdity of asking her how she was being furthest from my mind. The nurse explained that the tubes were drains and once they ran clear of blood, which could take up to a week, they would be removed. The intense pain was to be expected but I was concerned when she complained of difficulty in breathing. This didn't sound good news, but I assumed that it was all due to the operation which was understandable. The nurses, one in particular, kept coming and checking, monitoring her situation and giving her pain relief, whilst at the same time, his jokes were almost able to put a smile on her face.

These are her thoughts about the pain:

I was so tight-chested like I couldn't breathe without my chest cramping, it was so awkward and incredibly uncomfortable. I was certain I couldn't sustain the pain for much longer. I literally couldn't move let alone breathe. It just did not feel right, it wasn't a soreness that you'd expect. It was itchy, restricting and totally overwhelming.

Despite the monitoring and regular medication, Ellen still complained of pain. By the time Mr Charmingly-Direct checked up on her later that evening she had become distressed, to say the least. One side of her breast was feeling particularly painful, and she was convinced something wasn't right. Thinking he was just humouring her as he unwound the bandages, I caught the look of concern pass over his face and realised that my daughter was right. Her pain wasn't normal. A haematoma, a swelling caused by internal bleeding, had developed on one side of her chest and had to be dealt with post haste.

A terrible night's sleep followed for both of us, not least because she was in a lot of pain and I was beside myself with worry over this second, unexpected, operation. The night dragged on until morning eventually crept up on us both, when once again, she was whisked away to the operating theatre to have an 'evacuation of haematoma', of the right breast, and once again I stalked around the hospital feeling something more than worry. No flashing bricks were needed this time; the operation was just under two hours, during which time I phoned her dad to let them all know what was going on.

She was back on the ward again in no time and that area of her chest was now pain-free. She and I could breathe a sigh of relief or so we thought.

"Are you alright?" again, this stupid question. I suppose what I meant was had the pain gone? Desperate for her to tell me it had. "How are you feeling, has the pain eased? You don't look as though you're in pain."

She looked at me with her pale face and sad eyes and said nothing. I could tell she was trying to be brave. I so wanted her to tell me that there was no more pain, no more discomfort. Lady Luck, however, had a different plan. The pain was back, the same sharp, stinging sensation. This time though it was on the other side. Another visit, this time from the registrar, who confirmed it as another haematoma in the left breast. How did I feel? I was incensed. Could this be down to the fact that she was so bloody enormous by the time she finally got her operation? I wish I'd had the courage to ask but I just seethed silently.

Our friendly nurse kept coming to administer pain relief and attempted to cheer us both up but we were unable to fall under his charm. Managing to overcome my anger I was left not knowing what to think when they told me that she would have to undergo yet another operation to remove this other haematoma. I began to panic and wondered whether it was even possible to have three consecutive breast operations and successfully recover from them. I tried to be as positive and upbeat with her as I could but, honestly, what was there to say? It was completely out of my hands. She knew- we both knew, that to rid her of the pain another operation was necessary.

I made a second call to her dad, to let him know the not-quite-so-good news that she was having to go under the knife a third time and the reason for this was to remove a second haematoma. There wasn't a great deal he could say either, it had rendered us both speechless. He said to give her a big kiss from him and the boys and to let them know how it went and how she was. Even though they were all worrying and thinking about her, and their thoughts weren't always on the holiday it was better to be doing something fun. At least I hoped this was the case, anyway.

Instead of staying in the parents' room, the nurses had made a bed next to hers in the ward, so I could remain with her throughout the night.

Just like last time, the morning arrived slowly and for the third time in three days, I accompanied her to the operating theatre, kissed her and left her there once more for this second removal of the haematoma. To say I was in need of a little spiritual guidance, or any kind of guidance was an understatement. I had been recommended a book called 'Creative Visualisation'; what was there to lose? I sat in the parents' room, devouring all the pages related to healing and putting into practise some of the suggestions. I was past caring what anybody thought and closing my eyes tightly shut I chanted affirmations that she would get well and recover quickly. The helplessness I'd been feeling actually eased. Sending positive thoughts certainly wouldn't cause any harm and besides, it gave me something else to focus on.

I suppose the odds were that this would be the third and probably more to the point, hopefully, the final removal of a haematoma. Thankfully, it took less than an hour and the registrar who'd operated on her declared,

"I don't know what I've done but it's worked!"

Ellen was sitting upright in bed with no pain at all, and I didn't need to ask how she was. She said that for the first time since the breast reduction, she was able to breath properly and her chest felt so light. Good news indeed. She looked great, especially considering what she had gone through in the last seventy-two hours. Maybe, just maybe, Creative Visualisation works after all!

Mr Charmingly-Direct explained the importance of wearing supportive bras for the next few months. I understood that they were critical for my daughter's recovery but still, I cringed. Given our fraught experiences of bra shopping so far, the idea of diving back in made me incredibly nervous. Steeling myself, I knew it had to be done and I managed to order several sports bras fitting up to a D-cup and was relieved to find the process pleasantly easy.

She stayed in the hospital for a further eight days after this last operation. During the breast reduction procedure, the surgeon had removed from her small body 6kg of breast tissue, an incredible amount but considering her breast size, not surprising. This is the equivalent weight of an average, domestic cat or a gallon of paint. Small wonder she struggled to carry it all around with her. I still kept returning to my issue with size; she shouldn't have been left to grow so big. This amount was too big, simply too big for a twelve-year-old girl to deal with.

The rest of the family returned from their holiday looking disgustingly fit, healthy and sunburned which was in complete contrast to the pale girl lying in her hospital bed. Come to that, I didn't look much better. They were really pleased to see her and brought back some Alpine goodies for her and chatted about their ski adventures.

"Hello, hello," they all said in unison as they bustled into the ward, the boys kissed me and walked over to their sister, hesitating at the sight of her and the drips. She just smiled. "Skiing was good, lots of snow."

Conversation about the operation was limited, they might not have known exactly what she'd been through, but it didn't stop them from being glad to see her. Her Dad sat on the bed, looking and asking questions about the drips and everything else she was plugged into. This indirect conversation about all the paraphernalia surrounding Ellen was a lot easier than talking about haematomas, tissue and how did she feel.

Having them back acted like a real pick me up and she was quite happy to listen to their conversation whilst munching on the chocolate. Visiting hours were open so friends and family would troop in to see her at any time. For the first couple of days, she would just sit and listen to the conversation going on around her, not having the energy to participate. Thankfully, this was short-lived and soon she was chatting away with whoever popped in. It meant boredom didn't set in too often and the days went quickly. She also had frequent visits from our favourite rascally, bald and upbeat nurse, who I had decided to nickname Nurse Upbeat. He would always try to cheer her up and make her smile; often he would draw little smiley faces on her hands or knees. He was a tremendous pick-me-up for us both.

I stayed with her in the hospital for the first five days and then, as good as the parents' ward was, I really wanted my own bed and so I returned home in the evenings and came to see her first thing every morning. Ellen was a bit unhappy about this but I tried to explain that I would be back in the morning before she woke up and I would leave as late as she needed me to. I also felt that having a good night's sleep would help me to support her better the next day.

Over a week had gone by when the nurses finally removed the drains, a painful and sore process that elicited a lot of moans and groans. However, when the unravelling had finished and the bandages and the binder had been removed, it was then that she was able to finally see the results of her long-awaited operation. I held my breath as I waited for her response. There was absolute silence and then she smiled.

"They're cute boobs, Mum."

"Yes, they absolutely are!" I agreed joyfully, thanking everyone and anyone. Yay happy days were here again!

She was so pleased with the outcome, boobs that were a manageable size, D-cup and cute into the bargain. There was one drawback. They were only able to save one of her nipples, meaning only one of her breasts would have the ability to produce breast milk. Taking into consideration everything else, this felt like it was no big deal. She was very happy with her size, and it seemed a small price to pay. Circumstances do help us to learn how to be content with less.

Ellen left hospital after almost two weeks, bandages, binder, drains and stitches free, very glad to be home. The boys, in their own way, were very pleased to have her back. For the healing process to begin, she had to avoid stretching, strenuous exercise and heavy lifting, so any sports or games at school had to be avoided. This was to be expected and although she had previously enjoyed playing sports, it had been so long since she'd been able to do any physical activity that it was the least of her concerns. The only connection she'd have to sport for the time being were these sports bras which had to be worn 24 hours a day for eight to twelve weeks.

During the healing process, I relinquished all control over screen time, and she began to binge-watch a reality TV show. Of all the rubbish TV programmes out there, this was the one show I really couldn't get my head around. How could watching people you don't know doing things you don't care about possibly be of interest? When I finally questioned her as to its appeal, she admitted that it made such a difference to her to be the one who was watching for a change. She'd been looked at, studied, and examined for so long, and now it was someone else's turn. Ok, I got it.

As always, life had to go on, and not wanting to leave her alone, family or friends would come and look after her and she remembers feeling quite shy and embarrassed about the whole situation. At the risk of repeating myself, at twelve years old for her to be able to understand what had happened to her, let alone accept it was simply way beyond her years and far too distressing. They were very caring and kind and filled her days when I was working and couldn't be there.

Finally, after all the healing, her twelve-year-old life could now return to something resembling normality and from April she began to lead a life that a young girl should be experiencing, returning to school about seven weeks after the operation. This is a lot of school time in the life of a twelve-year-old to miss out on but, unfortunately, circumstances were such that there wasn't much we could do. Work was sent from school so that she could at least be able to keep up with her studies in some way but it didn't make up for the considerable amount of time that she was away from her friends and life in general. However, like a rubber ball, she bounced back and was soon involved with life. And much more than that, enjoying her 'cute boobs'!

10

The Weird and Wonderful!

Diary extract, 30th June 2008:

Four months after her breast reduction and because of all the stress of hospital appointments, I thought trying a different type of healing, a type of energy healing would be good for her. Also, I'm feeling a little down, as I'm very sad to say that even though neither she nor I have verbally acknowledged the elephant in the room, the fact is, it is noticeable that her 'cute boobs' have visibly, but only very, very slightly, begun to grow again. I just can't bring myself to say too much, if anything, about this. So, the plan to go to London, I suppose, could be a distraction on my part, not wanting to discuss what was happening all over again. It was too heartbreakingly sad and anyway they may stop, who knows.

"Mum, there's no way I'm going to have this appointment, I'm just not doing it."

"Look, let's just go to London, it's a lovely day, you can enjoy being somewhere other than school and we can find somewhere nice to eat. You never know, you may really enjoy it."

Yes, I had taken her out of school for this appointment, that's how keen I was for her to try it.

"I'll go to London but I'm not doing it!"

These were the words she spoke, in no uncertain terms, to me on the morning of the appointment. I wasn't going to be deterred, perhaps a little thick-skinned, I chose to ignore what she said. Although I have considerable faith in the medical profession, I do believe that complementary treatments have their place within the healing process. Energy healing is a branch of alternative medicine based on the belief that healers can channel and transfer energy into a patient and effect positive results for the mind, body and spirit. I'm all for positive outcomes and thought it would be good for my daughter to at least give it a go.

I'm always keen to try new things that may or may not make a difference and, after all, Creative Visualisation didn't seem to be a waste of time. I am also of the opinion that if you are unable to disprove something then you must consider that it might have some credibility. In my wisdom, therefore, I decided to make an appointment with an Energy Healer, who had been recommended by several different people. What had we got to lose? A day off school for Ellen. I worked part-time so that wasn't a problem; two return train fares to London and the cost of the appointment? As things turned out, I should have also included loss of face, although I didn't know it at the time.

My plan was to spend a day in London that would involve some sightseeing and a tasty lunch before the appointment. I didn't factor shopping into this equation because neither of us could muster up enough interest. It was four months after her reduction, and she had healed very well but still felt tired so the thought of battling with shoppers wasn't that appealing; not forgetting that shopping had also scarred us for life; no shopping was involved. However, it's funny, no matter how carefully something is organised it can still go wrong, best-laid plans and all that. The train journey was fine and with no further complaints from Ellen all seemed to be running to plan. The situation took a change for the worse during lunch, over a very tasty plate of salad. I chatted about the forthcoming appointment, reminding her that the specialist came highly recommended and summing up with,

"In any case, it has to be more calming and relaxing than the hospital appointments."

No answer came the stern reply. She had gone from being

monosyllabic to simply not uttering a word. This should have rung alarm bells with me but, as ever, my mindset was onwards and upwards and anyway, I'd been hoping that her lack of conversation and interest wasn't a reflection of how she was going to receive her forthcoming appointment. We finished our lunch and headed for that well-known part of London, Harley Street, famous for its number of private specialists in medicine and surgery.

It was a balmy, spring day and as we sauntered along streets lined with shops and restaurants, all felt right with the world, to me anyway. It soon became obvious that Ellen wasn't feeling my joie de vivre at all and began sulkily to lag behind. I was worried we wouldn't make the appointment on time but as we turned the corner, we were faced with these huge, impressive Georgian-style buildings, that was our destination. By this time, she was dragging her feet and any amount of encouraging on my part fell on obstinate ears.

We opened the large front door, which led into a long rectangular hall, at the end of which sat the receptionist. This was when the problem really started, with this nice, unassuming, receptionist who just happened to look a certain way and say all the wrong things, quite unintentionally I might add. My daughter took an instant dislike to her, became tight-lipped and refused to say a word, not that she had been saying a great deal during lunch or after for that matter. We were directed up a flight of stairs and instructed to fill out a form, whilst we waited for our appointment. Despite the atmosphere in the reception, the room upstairs was light and airy and had two sash windows overlooking a small courtyard. This gave me a little bit of confidence that all would be well. We sat by the window, and I filled out the form, while my daughter sat fidgeting and complaining on the edge of her chair. Two minutes later, the door opened and out came a very pleasant-looking man with sparkling blue eyes, who, like the receptionist appeared to be very kind and caring. I'm afraid not in my daughter's eyes. That's when she refused, point blank, to entertain any idea of taking part in this appointment and no amount of pleading and cajoling would work. She dug her heels in, yet again, said it wasn't for her and flounced off. All I could do was produce a nervous laugh, as she disappeared dramatically from the room. How I wished the ground could have swallowed me up.

Feeling foolish and embarrassed, I gathered what was left of my dignity and found myself spluttering,

"Well, it looks like you've got me then."

While certainly not standard practice, I think he could see how upset I was and how awkward this was for all concerned, so he simply ushered me into the consultation room. Recognising the situation for what it was, hopeless, she wasn't going to give in for all the money in the world, which this appointment was probably going to cost me, regardless of who attended the session or not.

He was thankfully sympathetic towards my situation and as I lay down on the couch, I tried in vain to stem the tide of tears. Sobbing, as I lay there, thinking how could she do this to me, why won't she just give it a try and the real dichotomy should I be worried about where she was now? Did I care? She'd be fine. Why was she so stubborn? This was for her benefit; it was all for her. So many mixed emotions were whirling around my head. He didn't ask too many questions, which I was glad about, and I received an hour of relaxation with soothing and calming meditation. I have to say it was the best experience, ridding me of all my negative thoughts and allowing me to let it all out. I hadn't realised how much upset I'd been carrying around. Without realising it, she had done me a favour and given me a chance to unburden myself and achieve some kind of mental stability.

All was not lost. However, at some point during the session, it did cross my mind that my twelve-year-old daughter could be wandering the streets of London on her own and that perhaps I should be a little concerned about this. I soon pushed those rather uncomfortable thoughts to the back of my mind and let myself slip into a trance-like state. What a neglectful, irresponsible mother I am.

Regrettably, after an hour, the session ended, and I was forced to go in search of my wayward daughter. She hadn't gone far and was waiting for me downstairs, trying her utmost to avoid eye contact with the receptionist. I floated into the room, feeling light and free as a bird and smiled sweetly at her. She was waiting for an angry comment and to be rebuked for stomping off. Too right, I had been angry and upset but that feeling had evaporated with the appointment.

"Ah, there you are. Have you been sitting here all this time?" My lack of apparent anger and concern took the wind right out of her sails. Pretending to be oblivious to her stony silence, I enthused about the experience, assuring her, "It was soooo relaxing. Such a shame you didn't fancy it."

I didn't say any more, realising that it wasn't the right time and that I should pick my battles with care. We travelled home in relative silence, she was lost in her thoughts and I, well I was still floating on my little cloud. I did eventually manage to persuade her to try again. While she was reluctant to start with, in the end, she had regular appointments, finding it very worthwhile. Giving her the chance to relax, she could aid healing from the inside and feel the importance of taking time out. See, Mum knows best.

On reflection, and in my daughter's defence, she had been through an enormous amount and to have yet another appointment, unnecessary in her eyes, was something she didn't want or need to go through, and she made that quite clear.

She said much later that she just wanted to be left alone both physically and spiritually. I suppose I should have taken this into account, you try as a parent to provide as much help and support to your children but sometimes you just can't get it right. Plus, the unspoken situation with her breasts which were beginning to grow certainly didn't help and no amount of unworldly guidance would do. She simply didn't want to be spiritually consoled.

11

Holidaying in the Land of the Free and the Home of the Brave

"And I pray, oh my God do I pray
I pray every single day
For a revolution."

Diary extract, 6th July 2008:

Life is giving with one hand and taking away with the other. We were so looking forward to getting away and taking the children to Disney Land, Florida. However, the elephant in the room can no longer be ignored, they are continuing to grow and show no signs of stopping. Life, for whatever reason, doesn't want to give her a break. Whatever higher power there was it certainly hadn't done with giving out hard lessons.

"Mum, have you noticed, look at them, just look!"

"I'm looking love, I'm looking. They have grown slightly but that might be it, they might just stop growing."

My comments fell on deaf ears. She was distraught by the obvious change to her breasts and cold panic gripped my chest. As I consoled her, all I could feel was a mounting dread. Over the last few years, my heart had been used as a pin cushion and every setback thrown at her felt like another pin digging in. I understood what was meant by the idiom 'to have a heavy heart', mine felt like lead. Why, oh why was this happening all over again? There was no answer; I was being brought to my knees with a love for my daughter and a situation that was way out of my control and one over which I had little choice. I had to pull myself together. What good would come from throwing my hands in the air, sobbing, crying and giving in? I was learning to squash my feelings and how I felt. Not even put a brave face on but just simply harden myself to the situation. It was the only way I knew how to cope and not show her how desperate I considered our position to be. If I gave in, where would that leave her? She needed someone to rely on, and to be that person, I had to be in control and deal with everything in a non-emotional way. Welcome to my world of being tough.

"Let's not panic, we don't know, they just might grow a little more and then stop." What was I saying? I could quite easily have been talking about a plant or tree but no, here I was talking about her breasts. "What we mustn't do is be worried about something that may well not happen." Did I believe this? I'm not sure I did but I was doing my best to reassure her and so I said, "To be on the safe side, I'll make an appointment with Mr Charmingly Direct as soon as we're back home."

"They're not my cute boobs anymore. I don't know what they are," she cried, deeply upset, giving inconsolable sobs. It was difficult to remain tough when faced with distress like this.

Ellen was right. There was no doubt that her D-cup boobs had vanished and it would seem that her breast tissue was once again on the rampage. Or maybe not? Maybe they would stop growing. Who really knew? Who was I trying to kid?

After surgery in February, her body cooperated and healed well. As a present to the five of us, we took off for Florida in July of 2008. It was a holiday with the sole intention of having fun and forgetting everything that had happened, allowing us all to move on and look forward to the future. It was a trip of a lifetime for the children, visiting Disney Land first and then a week spent on the beach. This holiday was something for us all to look forward to and more importantly experience together as a family. For too long my daughter had been in and out of hospital, travelling to and from appointments, seeing consultants and doctors, and displaying her top half to anybody that said they could help. It was now time for her, as well as the rest of us to forget all the angst that had gone on before and enjoy ourselves. She was not only wearing fun, fashionable swimwear for the first time as any girl her age should be able to enjoy, but she'd also actually enjoyed the experience of shopping for them, which was a complete contrast to the Topshop disaster. How liberated she felt not having to wear the large bra and oversized t-shirt attire.

We were looping the loop, riding the rapids and soaring through space. The children were old enough to wander around together and also the right height for nearly all the rides; this meant we didn't need to join them, and my husband and I could explore at our leisure, picking and choosing which rides we dared go on. I stopped short at the rollercoaster, simply looking at it made me feel queasy. Being wrenched around at high speed or plummeting to earth at a rate of knots was not my thing. In fact, I realised as I gazed up at it, that metaphorically speaking, the rollercoaster represented our lives, her life and the awful dread that it would all come crashing down on us. These words echoed in my mind: "As your daughter is very young, you need to know that there is a chance of further breast development after surgery. If this is the case, it may result in her…"

The second week on the beach and her perfect breasts had begun to grow again, with a vengeance. It was impossible to ignore. To say we felt crushed was an understatement. We were utterly shattered and my daughter was inconsolable.

I remember feeling so, so sad when it was obvious that they were continuing to grow but I just had to acknowledge it and park it. I also didn't like telling anyone or sharing how I felt with anyone. It wasn't that it was so embarrassing, but it was also admitting that they were, in fact, growing at a drastic rate and not only that but my recent scars were now being stretched. I just had to take it day by day and not think about the future or what it would hold. All I wanted was for them to be removed.

We continued the rest of the holiday putting on a brave face, being as positive as we could and doing our absolute best to enjoy ourselves, the very epitome of the stiff upper lip. There was absolutely no point falling apart and giving up, although that did cross my mind and to be honest the thought of what was going to happen next kept me preoccupied for the rest of the holiday. In all honesty, I struggled to put on a happy holiday face.

I remember reading or being told by some well-meaning person that it's not what happens to us that defines us but how we handle what happens; also, what doesn't kill us makes us stronger and worst of all, that God never gives you what you can't handle. Blah, blah, blah, all very philosophical. None of this erased the fact that my daughter was being used as a host by some overcharged, over-explosive, tissue-breeding parasite and there didn't seem a damn thing we could do about it. How does that define us or make us stronger?

We headed to Southwest Florida for the second part of our holiday. A long and sandy stretch of coastline, facing the Gulf of Mexico. We spent all our time swimming, snorkelling and going out for days fishing, or rather the boys did. Ellen and I would stay behind, swimming, sunbathing and collecting shells off the beach. Perfect.

But it was far from perfect, true perfection would have meant my daughter was holidaying with the same size breasts she'd arrived with. Was this too much to bloody well ask? This wretched little parasite was continuing to create havoc and her breasts even during the two weeks we were away, were being influenced and targeted by this freeloader. They had become, once again, a large melon size, fuller, drooping, verging on being very misshapen and hot to the touch. Dear God, please don't give me anything else you think I can deal with because I can't.

This holiday had now become reminiscent of the summer holiday in 2007, although the growth in her breasts hadn't quite reached the size she was then, at least not yet. This didn't stop those inappropriate looks and glances. She loved the water and would go with one or both boys to the pool. I found this out later on when she felt strong enough to tell me:

There was a dad and his son playing in the pool and all he did was stare in my direction. I was wearing my black swimsuit and I knew even when I had my back to him that he was looking. Weirdo, he made me feel really bad and I would wait until he wasn't looking to climb out of the pool.

People just can't help themselves, they're rude and ignorant and have no understanding of how to behave when they see bodies that differ from what is considered the norm. I should have at the very least, confronted him when I found this out.

There were other incidences which weren't perhaps as overt but still as violating. Her brothers, she knew, even at twelve years old, were oblivious to the subtle nods and winks. Her saddest comment was that she knew she was no longer a child. This statement is a very tough one to accept. It's a fact that every parent who has to witness their child suffering, suffers immensely and it was painful. But what was I to do? Go with her everywhere she went, stop her from going, tell the boys to watch out for salacious looks and stares? What exactly could I do?

Was it right that my daughter of twelve, going on thirteen years, considered herself no longer to be a child? I suppose as the urban dictionary calls it a 'twelve-teen', then maybe it is acceptable? The overriding issue, however, was what made her think that she was no longer a child? It was not because she was considered a young teenager but because of the sharp reality of her being dragged into an adult world, a place where she neither belonged nor wanted to be; the circumstances of this disease had turned her life upside down and around and around and certainly not for the better. She quite literally grew up too fast. Such a stark contrast, being sexualised before you've even started thinking about sex, while also being a medical mystery, having men leer at you while other men looked at your body completely dispassionately, surely this makes for extreme internal conflict.

I don't believe what was happening to her ruined our holiday, at least I'd like to think that this was the case, but it was, as I said, a very real and tremendous setback. In my mind, I was working on a list of questions for the appointment with Mr Charmingly Direct as soon as we were home. I felt reassured that, at least, we had this supportive professional, who we always seemed to turn to in our hour of need. If he hadn't been there, I'm not sure what we would have done. There just wasn't anyone from all the various appointments we had had that could help.

It was really important to find out whether there was any other way forward than the bombshell of an operation he had mentioned to us on our first visit. Just the memory of this made me feel sick, the feeling of dread was all-pervading. My thoughts had taken me to the horrific realisation that she didn't have a lot of choices open to her if her breasts continued to grow as they had previously and certainly seemed to be doing now. While I tried to ignore this depressing thought, there seemed to be no other option, at least no viable one. It was so dreadful to think that after everything she'd been through there was a very real likelihood it would all be repeated once more. The mental weight of going through the process again until the next surgery, which was more than likely going to be her final and most unwanted of all, was very heavy indeed. A bilateral mastectomy is a surgery in which both breasts are removed. It is most often related to breast cancer; this thankfully was not the cause of my daughter's condition, but it was a potential solution, nonetheless.

How was I going to approach this? Does she already have some idea? How will she feel and how do I feel? And what exactly will the long-term repercussions be of a mastectomy on a 12-year-old, prepubescent girl, both mentally and physically? I had no answers and wondered, once again, whether there was somebody up there having a laugh at our expense. It certainly felt like it. I knew the only way she was able to accept this was carrying on life through a foggy mental cloak of self-preservation. Not wanting to look and see too clearly.

Tough times were ahead again and deal with it I must.

12

Here We Go Again...

Diary extract, 21st August 2008:

This appointment was not supposed to happen. Her breasts should have remained the same size. Ok, we were warned but even so, no girl should have to go through this. Added to which, I can't even bring myself to write this, but another lump has appeared underneath her left armpit. Could the situation be any worse? I'm in total despair and Ellen, well, there are no words to describe how she's feeling.

No sooner had the wheels of the aircraft come screeching to a halt than I had booked a private consultation with our very understanding Mr Charmingly-Direct, who only six months earlier, had reduced my daughter's breasts to a perfect D-cup. Now all his good work seemed lost. They had grown back to size F and we desperately wanted to HALT, STOP things before they were back to their pre-surgery K/L-cup or, heaven forbid, any larger. Added to this was the possibility that another reduction wasn't a viable solution, and she would require something more drastic. So, it was with nearly inconsolable dread that we attended our appointment.

As always, Mr Charmingly-Direct gave us a warm welcome and was extremely sorry that her breast tissue had started to grow. Living up to his name, he candidly explained the very few options that were available to her. While he was extremely sympathetic about her situation, he did say that due to her age the possibility of regrowth had always been there. He went on to explain,

"I will need to refer her to London Children's Hospital, Great Ormond Street, for a further opinion to ensure that there are no avenues of treatment other than surgery."

We all knew, only too well, the surgery to which he was referring, the one that had always been there, lurking in the background like a monster in a horror movie. We pushed for viable alternatives and listened with mounting dismay as he went through the options. First, there could be another reduction surgery, followed by using Oestrogen blockers like Tamoxifen or Faslodex. However, while this may well prevent her breast tissue from growing there was the possibility that the blockers could affect bone density and damage her uterus. There were also serious concerns about using these in the longer term in someone of her age. The last thing we wanted was to cause any harm to other areas of her body, so this was off the list.

Next, he suggested having the reduction without any of the above but there was too much of a likelihood that her growth would happen all over again, as it had now. The uncertainty, the torment and the dread of whether or not they would grow again were too much to take. Another avenue closed.

Understanding and realising this dreadful situation was, to say the least, shocking, but there was another heart-wrenching anomaly hanging over our heads. Over the last couple of months, as well as her breasts continuing to grow, a lump had grown, ominously and gradually, underneath her left armpit. It was now the size of a tennis ball. After a careful examination, it was diagnosed as a lipoma in her left axilla. Again, the reasons were unknown. She had noticed this growth whilst on holiday but at that time it was very small and was fairly insignificant in comparison to her breasts. However, over the last month, it had, typically, grown dramatically and in unison with the increase in breast size.

This lump was almost like a third breast and was altogether too upsetting. It had left us completely stupefied. What on earth? What more could her breast tissue come up with to make her situation any worse? You had to admire her body's amazing ability to fight back against the reduction it had had to suffer. Was there no end to this tissue growth and what had caused it to branch out and start growing under her armpit? Give us strength.

We had been warned about the possibility of further growth after her breast reduction in February 2007 but not one person had even mentioned the possibility of a deviation from her breasts to under her armpit. I know her condition was rare, I understand that the professionals were baffled, but did no one in the medical world envisage this happening or foresee this as a possibility? We tried to find some humour, to laugh at the situation but it was impossible. I had the sort of crazy, maniacal laugh of a woman who had reached, yet again, her mental breaking point. How was my thirteen-year-old going to deal with three large lumps instead of two? How much of a brave face would she have to put on to get through each day? How uncomfortable was this tennis ball going to be underneath her armpit, as well as the weight of her ever-growing breasts? So many unanswered and truly awful questions.

It was necessary for her to begin again the continual round of tests and we had to make many, many visits to various hospitals, from September through to December. Just as before, there were a great many and I've listed a few of them below, as well as I can remember: Pelvic Ovarian Ultrasound scan, bone age and baseline DEXA scan, blood tests, oestrogen receptor studies and included in these appointments were visits to a consultant psychologist.

At the end of all this, the prognosis was, as expected, bleak. In a letter, Mr Charmingly-Direct delivered his recommendation,

"Further to my previous correspondence, I explained that on the basis of our BAPRAS (British Association of Plastic, Reconstructive and Aesthetic Surgeons) meeting, the preferred management from now on would be a bilateral mastectomy with consideration of reconstruction implants."

That was it, the final blow, no more hoping for a miracle. We had reached the sad realisation that there was no other path left open to her, she would have to undergo a double mastectomy, a radical and irreversible step, at the very young age of thirteen.

She hadn't even started her periods and both breasts were to be removed. Now that's mad.

My life had been turned upside down, shaken around and it still wasn't finished!

He also made it clear, as ever he was true to his nickname, that we had to realise this was an operation that would come with significant complications, especially wound healing and bleeding. My daughter was left in little doubt that not only was the mastectomy the only way to rid her body of any further growth, but it was not without its difficulties. Absolutely all her breast tissue needed to be removed.

The largest of the pins, in fact, it was a bloody great stake, had been slammed into my heart. God almighty, how did it all come to this? We can fly to the moon; we have satellite navigation and yet we have no idea why my daughter's breasts were growing at an incredible and unstoppable rate. There wasn't anything we could say or do, we were left floundering in a sea of misery. Her breast reduction operation wasn't without its problems, what exactly would she be in for this time around?

***

Looking back, on it, the period from June 2008, five months after her breast reduction, to June 2009 was, to put it simply, the worst in our family's life. We were going through the motions of attending appointments, discussing the best way forward, and trying to have some semblance of normality but in reality, we were all in a phase of denial. Life continued under a perpetual black cloud; it seemed that there was no weather pattern in this world that could send it on its way.

In February 2009 the size of her breasts was back to where it was exactly a year ago, before having the reduction but with the additional lump positioned underneath her left armpit. If I could have taken her place, taken on this condition myself, I would have.

At this time Ellen entered her adolescence, difficult enough at the best of times and began to experience extreme low periods, resulting in what she refers to now as self-sabotage. She would cut her own hair, not caring how it looked, and put colour on it, only to change it the following week. I would find clumps of hair blocking the sink or left abandoned on the floor and hair dye seemed to turn everything else that colour too. Her clothes were dull, in muted shades; I guess her intention was to look as anonymous as possible. I suppose these were situations where she could be in control. When her size became too enormous, changing her hair colour and style and the way she wore clothes was all she could do which was in some way linked to being a young teenager. Indeed, they were the only avenues open to her that gave her any kind of say or power over her teenage self. She was in effect competing for control of herself with the parasitic host that had laid claim to her breasts. It was a contest that she wasn't ever going to win until her Juvenile Gigantomastia had been conquered and eradicated.

At thirteen years old, she had officially become that teenager who sulks, rants and raves but even these emotions were stymied by one huge difference, instead of a gradual physical growth into womanhood, her female physicality had launched itself upon her in a very short space of time. It was a given that her teenage normalcy was shaped and moulded by her experience of what had happened in the last abysmal years of trauma and by what was yet to come. How were we as parents going to deal with this and how was she, as a teenager going to do the same?

I foolishly carried out some research on adolescence and found some interesting and worrying information: "Adolescence is a very vital period that determines how a person will view and interact with the world as an adult. The stress you experience through puberty can shape your brain and determines the person you will become. Adolescence involves an intricate mix of genetic and environmental factors that contribute to individual patterns of personality change. Many types of stress can come with the territory of being a teenager." (Christian Jarrett,

Psychologist)

Unfortunately, my daughter was under a monumental amount of stress and this wasn't just the type of stress that comes from being a teenager. How, exactly, was this going to shape her brain and determine the characteristics she would have as an adult? I had to recognise that, whether I liked it or not, what she was going through would change the person she would become. I also discovered that emotional support can help to combat a cycle of negative personality change during adolescence. (Christian Jarrett 11/06/18). It is vital as a parent to focus a great deal of attention to provide support and help nurture their personalities. Keep channels of communication open!

I know parenting means pointing them in the right direction, showing by example, providing an emotional prop and ultimately unconditional support. I tried very hard to do all this but as any parent knows, your best isn't always enough. Her social life was curtailed; it was difficult for her to fit in and behave normally when what came before her dictated what she could do, and how and where she went. On the odd occasion when she did go out, it worried me. I was concerned about her feelings and how she would deal with many of the pitfalls that may arise, boys, clothes, stares and failure to fit in and be normal.

She ultimately turned to her two pet guinea pigs, Honey and Popsy, for solace. I think they were more of a lifeline than anything else. She could tell them anything without judgement. She would lie down on her bed and her favourite guinea pig, with its gorgeous honey-coloured fur would sit on top of her chest grooming, squeaking and licking itself.

When I knew my mastectomy was going ahead, I remembered thinking that I wouldn't be able to balance both my guinea pigs on my chest – hands free. This thought triggered more thoughts of the necessity of saying goodbye to my large breasts. They were a part of me, even if they were an unwanted part. I thought it was necessary to acknowledge the fact, that they would very soon, be gone forever. I had thoughts of loss and fear surrounding this irreversible procedure. I knew it was the right decision but intuitively my mind and my body naturally did not want to part.

Her days at school were difficult, no two ways about it. She had gone back after the summer holidays with breasts that once again were almost the size she had been before the reduction. Who was going to understand this, let alone believe what was going on? It was bad enough the first time around for her, of course, but also for the boys. Children can be so hurtful and her younger brother has said that he was bullied by classmates who would make nasty comments and rude remarks about her. At the age of ten, it was hard for him to understand and left him feeling sad, helpless and isolated. I just dreaded thinking about all three of them going through their own private torment. It was unbearable.

The changing rooms at school were awful, it was uncomfortable to get undressed in front of your peers, who all wore bras of a normal size. The conversation would always be about clothes, bras and boys, there was nothing I could contribute that any of them would understand. I couldn't get used to my chest size, as it was always changing, everyone around me seemed curious to know what was happening but not brave enough to ask me. On one occasion, I mentioned having to take off my top when I went to the doctors and they were shocked, so I didn't bother telling or unloading again, after that. It became exhausting plotting ways of hiding them, whilst feeling permanently self-conscious. The thing was, I didn't even know what was really happening myself.

Where was this so-called pastoral care from the school? It was so needed, not only for my daughter but for my sons. At the beginning of the Autumn term, I wrote a letter explaining in far more detail everything that had happened over the last 20 months. I requested that the school be a little more lenient with her on the day-to-day grind and also give a nominated female member of staff to whom she could go at any time of the day. We received the following response,

"…to have her as the only person who is not tackled on these things would draw further attention to her which we are keen to avoid. I am also sorry you feel that pastoral care at our school is not readily available… Perhaps it is the change of key stage and having a male assistant head that is the issue here."

Um, could be, what do you think?

The letter continued, "We have certainly given feedback to staff about your daughter's condition, but I am happy to reinforce that with them now that the school year has begun."

Now, dear readers, can you think back to a certain time in my daughter's school life when a harridan of a female teacher asked her what she had stuffed up her jumper? Me thinks the Head Teacher is telling porky pies!

Unfortunately, the reality was that it didn't matter how much I ranted and raved about everything, nothing could detract from the awful fact that she had grown, yet again, to an enormous size and the mastectomy had to go ahead. The pictures just before the mastectomy are on the following page; even though I have lived and breathed this disease, these graphic photos still manage to shock and distress me. Have a care when looking at them, they really aren't pleasant and should perhaps carry a PG warning.

I continue to have nervousness about these pictures being looked at in ways that do not fit into the context of this story and falling into the wrong hands. I consider this was and is the overwhelming and serious issue associated with Juvenile Gigantomastia, the problem of being taken as an opportunity for sexual and even pornographic gratification. For example, if you research books about 'Gigantomastia', the results are books that are about women who happily flaunt and love their very real large breasts. I might be exaggerating, and I have, thankfully, no personal proof, but I'm under no allusion as to the possible effects of these pictures when seen by certain perverse people in society.

My daughter, at such a young age, was so aware of the negative looks, making her feel exposed and extremely uncomfortable and knowing that in some way there was a sexual connotation connected to the stares. I have to reiterate that this is a very real female condition and because it is linked to a girl's sexuality it is seemingly considered less of a problem. Don't all women want big breasts? Added to the fact that her condition was for the most part dealt with by male consultants, most of whom were extremely good, who, because they don't have breasts, cannot hope to empathise nor understand the severe emotional rollercoaster associated with the disease. While there were thankfully few, there were doctors and consultants along the way whose approach and way of dealing with her made her feel so much worse. That said, our favourite Mr Charmingly-Direct remained in our eyes, "Top of the Pops!"

So, very, very sadly, it was back to the same hospital, to the same children's ward and most probably the same theatre for an unthinkable operation for a girl thirteen years old.

12A
Hospital Photographs

The abnormal and enormous, (size unknown, because buying any more bras was a thing of the past), with the lump underneath her armpit, just before the Mastectomy, 2009 aged thirteen years

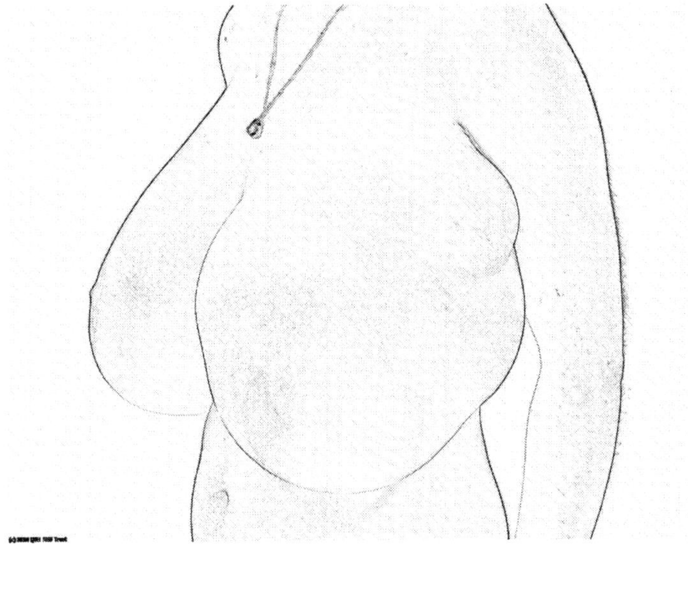

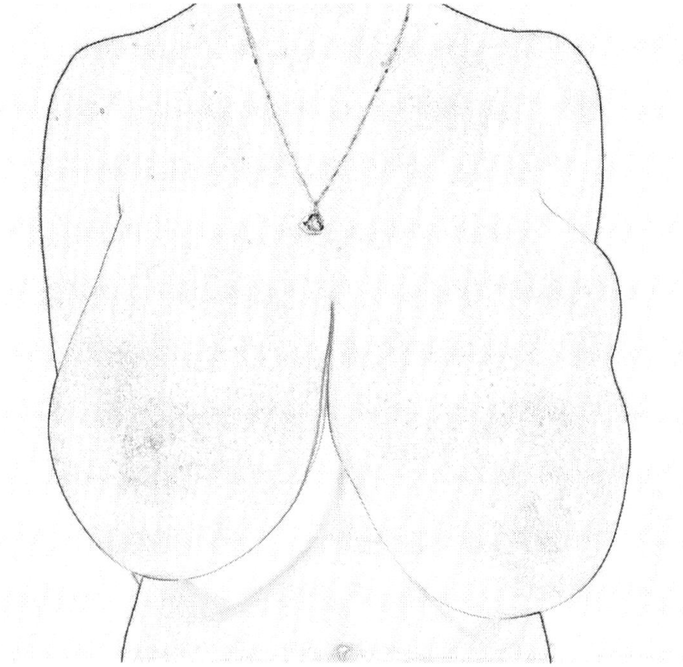

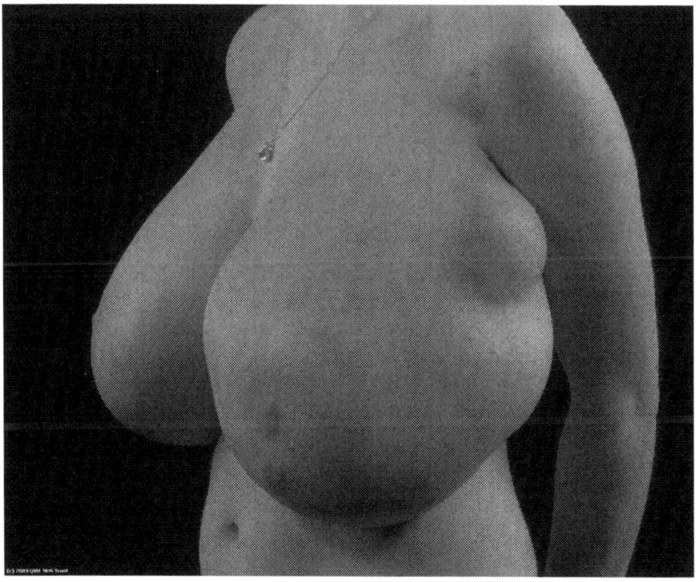

Aged 13 years.

13

A Double Dose of Sadness

Bilateral Mastectomy on a Children's Ward: Age 13 years.

"And so I cry sometimes
When I'm lying bed
Just to get it all out
What's in my head
And I, I am feeling a little peculiar."

Diary extract, 5th June 2009 – Déjà vu:

Writing this in the morning as there will be no time later, I don't think. I stayed overnight in the parents' ward and didn't get the best night's sleep. Too busy worrying but I should be used to it by now. The big 'M' op is happening today and, as if to add insult to injury, it's also my youngest son's 12th birthday. Don't you just love these coincidences? I'm experiencing a rollercoaster of emotions – glad that all the worry of continued growth will be gone but incredibly saddened for her having an operation that will rob her of a natural-looking female form, give her visible scars and remove both nipples and areola.
My emotions are all over the place.

I had been told that this would be yet another lengthy operation. So here we were, heading to the operating theatre, me holding her hand as they wheeled her along, feeling what exactly? Constant heartache, gratitude, relief, dread, I just didn't know. Leaving her in their capable hands, I was back in one of the hospital's cafes, having yet another coffee, my loyal brick-like pager my constant companion. I focussed my thoughts on anything other than what might be happening to her and how I felt; in fact, thinking was not a good idea. I had planned ahead this time and arranged to meet a friend for lunch, which would act as a distraction and help me pass the time. I couldn't cope with the constant clock-watching and the possibility of giving in to my disquieting contemplation. Distraction was key.

I ditched the pager as its range only reached just outside the hospital grounds, grabbed my handbag and off I went. No criticism please about wining and dining whilst my daughter underwent a life-changing operation. I had to eat and it was only four hours into her operation. We met for an hour and although I didn't feel hungry, I chomped my way through some tasty tagliatelle. I do remember thinking as I was sitting in the restaurant, that I must surely be the only person there whose thirteen-year-old daughter was undergoing a bilateral mastectomy. Luckily, it's difficult to choke on pasta.

I left the restaurant weighed down with worry, a full stomach of pasta and a glass of wine, fortification of some kind was very much needed. Walking back through the park to the hospital I broke into a run, I just wanted to run away from it all. I wasn't allowing myself to feel much and the feeling I had was of being emotionally flat, everything was flat, my mood, the weather and most probably, by now, my daughter's chest. I had the urge to chant and moan in a similar way to native Americans, throwing my hands in the air, stomping heavily around a campfire and offering prayers to whatever God was listening. If there was a God, which I was pretty certain by now that there wasn't, I had this real urge to shout to anyone and everyone in the park,

"Guess what? My thirteen-year-old daughter, she's having a mastectomy. What do you think of that then? What do you think?"

Looking at young girls, I wanted to warn them, "You be careful, just take care – there's a nasty disease on the rampage that will literally eat you up!"

Without a doubt, this was a moment of madness and although I needed to let off steam, I was conscious that it wasn't going to happen here in this park. Hold the urge, hold that urge. I slowed to a fast walk, taking deep breaths, in, out, in, out, but this wasn't working and I felt an irresistible need to laugh hysterically. Was I going completely mad? I read somewhere that laughter is our consolation prize for consciousness. Yes, that sounds about right. It took an enormous amount of effort to squash these feelings, but I managed and thankfully my short outbreak of madness came to nothing, and I continued my dispirited walk back to my situation normal. With my brick in the hospital, I wandered the countless corridors, numb to what was going on around me, trying not to analyse how and why we had arrived at this fateful day. I felt uneasy and impatient with all the walls, rooms and hustle and bustle of the hospital. I couldn't remain within these confines, outside had to be an improvement.

Surprisingly, the sun was still shining and people walking by were still smiling. Her situation, I surmised, could be a whole lot worse. It wasn't all that bad, surely? Fleetingly, my feelings about her situation would raise their ugly head but I was becoming adept at burying them deep into the recesses of my mind. Concentrate on a happy and positive outcome and a successful operation, free of difficulties and the need for any further medical intervention. And then the rollercoaster of emotion would unleash itself; but why did this happen to her, to our family, why, why? I know we cannot choose who our children will be or what will be their fate, but this was something so startlingly, ridiculously unexpected and abnormal. Keep it together, bury, bury, submerge those thoughts.

It was late in the day, the sun had stopped shining and it was probably never going to come out again when, eventually, a nurse came to tell me that the operation had gone well and that I could go and see her in the recovery ward. It was done!

Relieved that the waiting was over and overwhelmed with worry, I arrived in the recovery ward, to an extremely distressed little girl, who was in a great deal of pain.

"The pain is so, so incredibly awful. I feel like my flesh has been ripped off and then torched, and the weight on my chest is unbearable. Please take the pain away," she moaned, her words coming out in short bursts.

Her moaning tore through me like shards of glass and my nerves were in shatters. OH Please! She was beside herself with excruciating pain and I was beyond holding back the tears. I frantically looked around to ask someone, anyone, to give her more pain relief. She wouldn't let me leave and under no circumstances was I allowed to put her arms back down on the bed. As soon as her arms were lowered, she was in pain and the poor nurse, who with heroic patience was holding her other arm, should have been off duty over half an hour ago. Her pain was made worse when she laid her arms flat on the bed and so my job and the nurse's job, for however long it took, was to hold them up and away from the bed.

I don't know if the pain in her arms was due to their position, which had possibly been placed over her head for the whole of the ten-hour operation, but they were certainly objects of agitation and distress for her. I managed to stop a nurse in her tracks, the recovery ward was busy and trying not to yell or appear too distressed, I requested that she be given:

MORE PAIN RELIEF, PLEASE!

"She really is in a lot of pain, is there anything more you can give her?"

"I'll see what I can do, but she has already been given some."

"Oh, ok, it's just she seems so distressed."

"Well, she has just had an operation."

"Yes, yes I realise this, thanks."

I was too distraught to respond to such a comment. Busy or not please be a little kinder. Helpless, apart from being able to hold her arms, I gave in to a few more tears. I was prepared to stay there the whole time, if need be, holding her arm, or arms now, because the dutiful nurse had left the building.

My own arms were now burning with pins and needles but finally, finally, as the morphine she had been given began to take effect, she could be wheeled into the children's ward. I gave in to a huge sigh of relief. Very gradually, she became calmer, she was drifting in and out of drowsiness. I sunk down next to her and with her arms now flat on the bed, held her hand. I allowed myself to close my eyes, musing over the strange events leading up to this point and wondering, once again, how on earth we had ended up here. If somebody had said to me after the birth of my daughter, that I would be sitting on my 13-year-old daughter's hospital bed, after she had a surgical operation to remove both breasts, plus a tennis ball which had formed underneath her left armpit, I wouldn't have been able to believe them. A profound sense of sorrow came over me and I didn't think either of us would ever be the same again.

Trying to be pragmatic, I reasoned that both her boobs and the ball were being dictated to by this unstoppable host-parasite, which was set on swallowing her up, so as drastic as it was, this must surely be the best of situations. She certainly didn't want to spend any more time with that part of her body which was set on taking over her entire life and whether we liked it or not, this takeover bid that her breasts were attempting had been stopped. Her breast tissue had been completely vanquished by this operation, no more tissue. What a strange and unpredictable world we live in and, as we found out, sometimes medical science just doesn't have the answer.

Nurse Upbeat, who'd been such a comfort following the reduction surgery popped in to see her. Ellen was asleep, probably still in her morphine-induced state but I knew she'd be pleased that he'd made the effort. She loved this nurse; he was a ball of positive energy and could make us both laugh. Something that was very much needed.

She says:

I remember him sitting with me after my reduction, watching television on the ward, and the news broke that Michael Jackson had died. He was never without something to say, and he just talked to me about this breaking news, not expecting me to provide an answer but just discussing it anyway. What he said, I can't remember, and it didn't really matter, it was more that he would spend time talking to me.

Only this nurse and having her cute D-cups back were all that could put a smile on her face.

It was the very next day, after her mastectomy operation, that I was informed she was a bit of a 'bleeder'; apparently, some patients are. Could it have something to do with the vast amount of tissue that had been extracted from my daughter's chest? Just a thought and one that on many occasions I have mooted, the issue of size versus time. Losing a great deal of blood during her ten-hour ordeal meant she needed a blood transfusion. This is a common, safe medical procedure in which healthy, matching donor blood is given to the patient through an intravenous line. All very straightforward, or at least it should be, unfortunately, the blood that was given to my daughter, although it was the same blood group, caused her antibodies to form a response and attack the red cell protein in the blood, for whatever reason, causing an allergic reaction and her skin became red and itchy. She was given antihistamines to reduce the allergy.

Given Ellen's past medical history, this was no surprise, she was allergic to many things, and this was yet another of a long list. If for some reason, however, she needs another blood transfusion in the future, then the donated blood should not contain this red cell protein, for which she now has an antibody. With me so far? I was struggling at this point. Therefore, she needs to have a National Blood Service Antibody card, which provides all the important data. "Oh right, yeah, ok, thanks!" Believe me, receiving this information, just after her operation, put my head in a complete spin! For goodness' sake, am I going to remember this?

Here she was back in the children's ward once again and this time there was no further surgery needed, but the operation had left her feeling incomparably sore, tired and unable to sit up easily, so lying down was her go-to position. To break the monotony of the four walls we both felt that the ceiling in the children's ward should have been painted and decorated with some cartoon characters or anything that children could look at whilst they were lying flat on their backs, and that would relieve the boredom. We would spend whole afternoons, deciding what kind of art would work, and we even mentioned it to Nurse Upbeat. He thought it was a good idea and told us to get painting, that's as far as we got.

"Right, it's time for your walk, time to get out of bed, lazy!"

The unenviable job of encouraging her to walk around for a few minutes, several times a day, was mine. As much as we understood it would help her in the recovery process, trying to coax a grumbling daughter into walking, while also being mindful of the IV tubes, wires and poles that came along for the ride, was no mean feat.

"Leave me alone, I don't feel like getting up."

"Come on, I'm sure you must feel like going to the toilet, it's been ages since you last went?" I had formed a cunning plan and tried to time her walks with visits to the toilet.

"Oh, for goodness' sake, mind my tubes and don't touch my arm there, it hurts," she replied bitterly.

"Ok, ok, I'm trying to be as careful as I can."

I raised my eyes to the ceiling, banking on the fact that she wouldn't see and took a deep breath. Patience, they say is a virtue. It was a juggling act trying to get all the tackle into the toilet with her, whilst still allowing her some privacy. I had to continuously remind myself that there was no rush, we had all the time in the world and that she was still recuperating. Sometimes, she would leave it to the very last minute, resulting in an awkward dash to avoid any accidents. I was learning, learning to remain calm, to keep a fixed smile on my face, getting angry or upset just wasn't helpful.

These are my memories and observations and Ellen, quite rightly, has her own thoughts and recollections:

Staying in hospital was hard and the nurses had to wake me up on an hourly basis to check up on me and give me my revolting medication. So, sleep was vital, which was all I wanted to do but was consistently interrupted. I also had to wear tight-fitting long, compression socks, because as I was practically bed-bound, they helped enhance my blood circulation. They were incredibly tight and uncomfortable and then add this to the fact that from the waist up I was in agony.

I felt like I'd been in a car wreck. Battered, bruised and very fragile, all I wanted was sympathy, not medication. Sleeping, when I was allowed, was on my back due to the drips, tubes and drains that prevented me from moving.

Being woken up at 4 am to take some pills when all I could just about do was turn my head was awful. I felt like a corpse and just wanted the nurses to leave me alone. Several times I would refuse to take the tablets and the nurses would sometimes struggle with my refusal. I always appreciated being given an explanation as to why and what the tablets were for. My favourite nurse was far more understanding and rather than the usual blackmail - the sooner you swallow these the sooner you can sleep - he explained what they were all for as well as giving me a bit of sympathy.

There were times when I got quite lonely, particularly when I was unable to fall back to sleep after swallowing these giant tablets. I don't remember watching a great deal of television or looking at my phone. I do remember one text from a friend sharing some juvenile gossip with me, but still avoiding the taboo subject of what I was currently going through. Which just confirmed how little understanding my peers had.

I suppressed a lot of emotions throughout this time, and I no longer looked in the mirror, as I didn't need a reminder of how I looked – particularly prior to my operations. Isolation seemed the safest option and whether it was at school, where I would spend the time in the library or at home absorbing myself in a television show. I didn't blame people for not understanding or relating to it, but I equally didn't have the patience for juvenile chit chat, so I just removed myself and found it easy being left alone.

There was more complaining but understandably so when it was time for the drains to be removed. This was a definite step forward towards recovery, but as this was her second time around and being almost an expert in breast surgery, she knew what she was in for. It's a similar situation to childbirth: the first time around you don't have much idea of the pain factor. The second time you know exactly what to expect and knowledge can be a dangerous thing. Removal of the drains is painful and as they are being pulled out it can be agonising because part of the skin, which has begun to heal around the tube, must be broken. Not pleasant when they continue to be tugged at regardless of how the patient feels. The longer the drains are left in the chest, the more painful the procedure. Ellen wasn't happy at all. At one point she stubbornly refused to let them do any more tugging, but they simply had to come out. Neither I and certainly not the nurses were going to give in.

Just as before, friends and family came to visit. It was important for her to see some different faces and a change of conversation; seeing me all the time wasn't so much fun. It also meant that I could be relieved of my duties and give somebody else the toilet dash, the drug request, the bed bath and the fluffing and reshaping of pillows; not easy when the hospital pillows tended to be lumpy and solid. Deja vu, with flashbacks to 2008.

I wonder whether we were judged for going ahead with this operation and if so, I would like to know how big is too big? At what point do you say enough is enough, that my daughter's body and mind are unable to take the strain of watching a part of her grow, yet again, to an indeterminate and more than likely, hugely unacceptable size? Her slight body frame, not to mention her state of mind just couldn't endure another increase from the perfect size D-cup to the horrifying K/L or even larger, because there was no way of telling how big they would grow and when the nightmare would stop. Nobody was able to tell us because the medical world just didn't know. It was with an enormous amount of sadness and an overwhelming feeling knowing that as parents we had somehow let her down and failed her. Nobody wants to agree to an operation that strips a young girl of part of her femininity but what option did we have? Our hands were tied.

The consultant had also stressed that it was of paramount importance that all the breast tissue was removed during the procedure, otherwise any left behind, no matter how small, would start to grow again. Above all else, this highlighted the unpredictability of her breast tissue and the insidious way that it randomly multiplied. This fact was the overwhelming and deciding factor to go ahead with the mastectomy. It was the determining factor. The operation had been planned and explained to us in detail and although there was an enormous amount to take in, it was some comfort to know that she was in extremely good hands.

I did, however, have reservations about the tissue expanders that would be put in during the procedure, after all the breast tissue had been removed. These are temporary implants that are gradually over many weeks, inflated with saline to stretch the skin and muscle, until it reaches the desired breast size. My concern was the very real possibility of her reacting allergically to these silicone implants, my reasoning was simply based on her history and her allergy to latex. My concern was slightly eased by a friend who worked as an allergy specialist, who assured me that there is no cross-reaction between latex and silicone, even though there is no test which can prove or disprove an allergy to silicone. Nothing is straightforward. In the end, there was no option available other than to put in expandable silicone implants. It was a fait accompli and, as it turned out, she suffered no adverse reactions. That's a first.

Following the operation, she was left with a completely flat chest; no 'cute boobs' that she would be taking home. Having no chest at all is easier to deal with than having two gigantic breasts and a tennis ball. Call it what you want, encumbrance, impediment, burden or hindrance, once she had healed, she was free from it all. She had a blank canvas. At the age of thirteen she could now begin the journey to discover and experience what having normal-sized and shaped breasts, ones that would remain more or less the same size, was all about. Not a lot to ask for and so from this traumatic surgery there came a defining moment in my daughter's life, freedom.

13A

Photos On The Wild Side

Hospital photographs of tissue removed after the Mastectomy, 2009, aged thirteen years.

I was in two minds about whether to add some photographs of the mass of tissue that was my daughter's breasts, which include the revolting add-on to her problems. I have decided to spare you the reader no mercy. If for any reason you really are squeamish, I advise you to refrain from looking, it's not a pleasant sight.

Some people give names as a term of endearment for a strange or unusual growth that they may, unfortunately, have. For us, the add-on lump underneath her armpit became known as the tennis ball, it looked, in shape at least, very much like one. The tennis ball and its accompanying playmates, the left and right breast are photographed together and the other photo is of the left breast and the tennis ball. The ruler next to the mass gives an indication of the size and amount of tissue that was extracted. I never found out the amount in weight - a lot! They lay exposed, looking like an aggressive alien mass, which was thankfully removed and is now finally divorced from any part of her body. It is an extremely beastly sight, so once again, care should be taken, viewing is not for the faint-hearted.

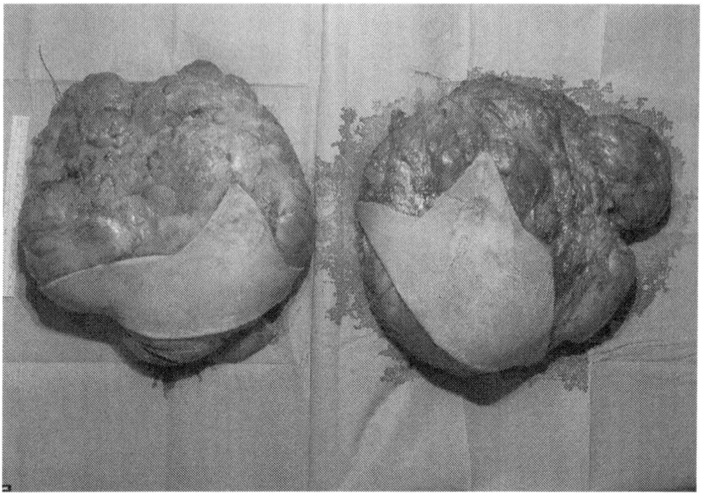

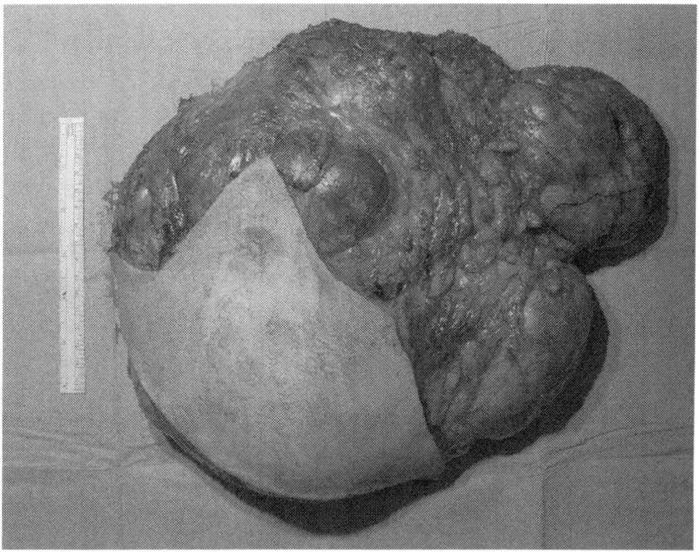

14

Two Plus Two

I would like, just for a moment, to interrupt my daughter's stay in hospital and consider the various possibilities that her disease could have brought about. A pause for thought, if you like.

As you know, I had many, 'what if' moments and I began to wonder what would have happened if nothing had happened?

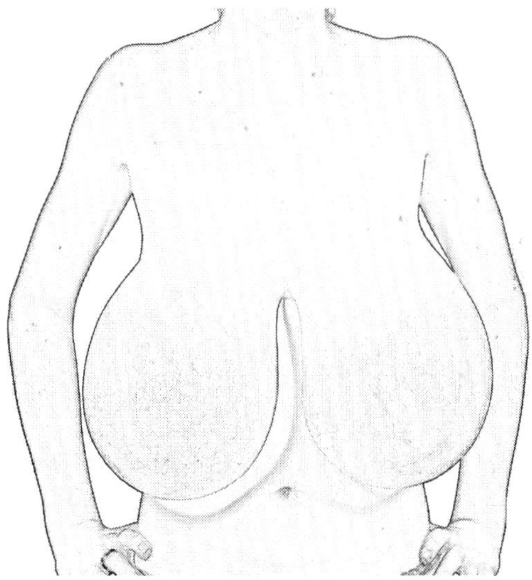

2008

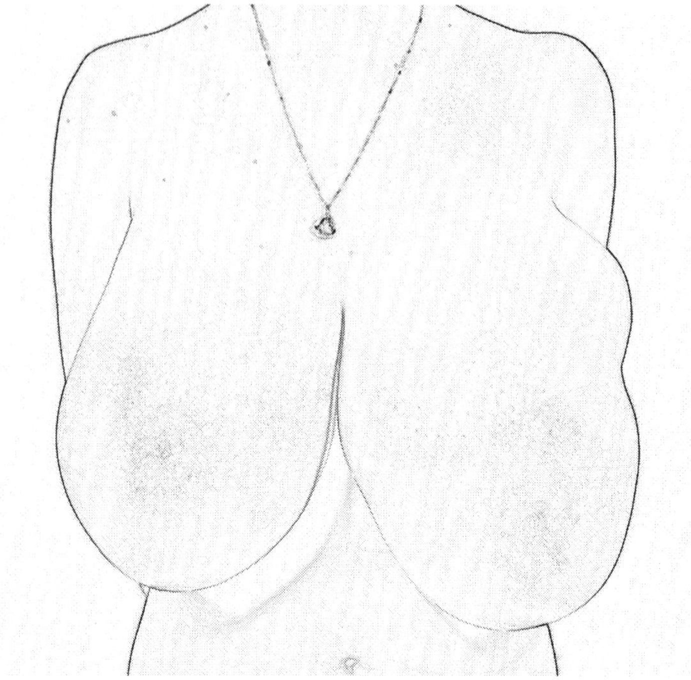

2009

My thoughts took me down this route: If you take the amount of breast tissue which grew from 2007 to 2008, just before her breast reduction, and added it to the explosion of tissue from 2008 to 2009, before her mastectomy, all the while considering that she was only 13 years old, how big would she have been by the time she reached full maturity if nothing had been done? This is of course not to mention the unusual, extra lump that had appeared under her left armpit. Would this too have continued to grow? How much more difficult would it have been for her to move around? What awful size would they have become until they stopped? And would they have stopped? There are so many 'what ifs' and unanswered questions.

I also wonder if there are girls out there, right now, in similar situations that for whatever reason are unable to do anything to put it right. It's quite horrifying to think about and unrealistic to believe that Ellen was or is the only girl in the world suffering from Juvenile Gigantomastia. My wonderings took me to a decision that, as we were unable to find anybody or any support groups that could help us when we so badly needed some help, I should be that person who sets up a website or provides a contact to support similar sufferers. It's surely got to be worthwhile, even if we just help one person that's preferable to nobody.

***

Since all this has happened, I have become almost obsessed with programmes dealing with medical and physical problems and similar situations. It's akin, in fact, to why Ellen liked and still does like watching 'Big Brother', where the sole purpose is to watch other people live together, where she could lose herself in their lives, watching instead of being watched.

On occasions, therefore, and much to my daughter's horror because she finds watching other people's physical disabilities too distressing, I watch an American reality television series, 'Botched' where two of California's best Plastic Surgeon Consultants put right surgeries that have gone wrong or try to help improve the physical appearances of a patient. Many of their patients come to them in the hope of correcting previous breast operations or simply to increase their bust size by having breast implants, very few want to decrease their size. Although, I could think of someone who was desperate for that.

Whilst watching one episode, a woman, who was there for butt implants but who also had extremely large breasts, size L-cup didn't come anywhere near to representing the size she was and these, she admitted, were increased on a regular basis at home, using a DIY method of injecting saline into expandable implants. This was a similar procedure to the one Ellen will have to undergo after having her expandable implants put in place after her mastectomy.

I was, quite frankly, appalled. Why would you want to keep increasing the size of your bust, let alone do it yourself? What is it that makes women want bigger and bigger breasts? Is it society imposing its own ideas, culturally reflecting the idea of female beauty? In 2013, a paper by Viren Swami and Martin Tovee found that preferences for larger breasts were significantly associated with greater tendencies towards "benevolent sexism", expressed by emphasising men's role to protect and provide for women in exchange for women's compliance to traditional gender roles. As well as objectification of women. Why then would this encourage women to want bigger breasts? One key finding from a host of studies of female breast size is that men predominantly prefer medium size, not large breasts. "Across the cultures, men do not consistently prefer large breasts." Therefore, "the motivation seems to be a woman's own perception of her body image rather than any other influences," (Psychology Today online. Jan 14th 2020).

As I continued to watch, it became apparent that the size which she had reached, by injecting saline, was most probably the same as amalgamating the two pictures of my daughter, above. This woman's breasts were truly, abnormally and comically bizarre and you must question the psychology of a person who actively, out of choice, increases her breasts to such a size. She enjoyed being the centre of attention, giving cause for people to stand, stare and even take photographs of her; morbidly weird. The outlandish reason she was on the programme was to have implants put in her buttocks so that the size of her backside would resemble her breasts, I kid you not. Maybe these implants would act as a counterbalance, who knows and who cares?

I was very reassured when both surgeons refused to put implants into her backside, saying that the butt is designed to take on a lot of weight and stress and no implant would ever stand the stresses created daily by the bottom. Anyway, I'm digressing and should stick to the topic but as you can quite clearly see I was left dumbfounded by this cavalier approach, but it takes all sorts of people to make the world go around.

I think if my daughter's breast tissue had been left to grow uninterrupted it would have been impossible for her to stand upright if at all, as the weight at the front would have been too much. Maybe then, the sole purpose of the butt implant, by the saline, self-injecting woman, was to act as a counterbalance after all? It's a thought.

***

Both bouts of growth before the mastectomy and the physical difficulties they brought with them have been touched upon but one thing I haven't mentioned is the way it affected how my daughter walked. Walking up and down stairs became more awkward and on one occasion, she missed her footing and fell down four concrete steps, the weight of the top half of her body causing her to land very heavily on her knees. She still remembers how she cried with pain and shock. The impact would not have been anywhere near as bad if she hadn't been so top-heavy. For a long time, the little things we take for granted like running just weren't possible. Her breasts were massive and burdensome and got in the way and her only way of moving quickly was to try and walk fast. As a result, she adopted a different style of walking, a noticeable gait, bent slightly forward, the stoop was a way of hiding them because the weight was dragging her down. Her arms were fixed slightly in front and pushed into each side of her chest. This was to stop their movement, to hold and support them and thereby alleviate some of the weight.

Even after all the removal of tissue, she continued to walk in this manner; I think it had become a habit and a safety mechanism. I have mentioned it to her more recently and she still says that she had no idea that she walked in this way and that it was so noticeable. Whilst thinking and writing about the way she walked for this book, I read an article by Christian Jarrett, 2016, from BBC Global News, online:

"We often think we can read someone's personality from their gait – but while many of these assumptions are wrong, your walk may nevertheless reveal the one thing you are trying to hide."

This was so true for Ellen, by leaning forward and clenching her arms into her chest she was able to walk almost normally whilst trying to cover up the two things she very much wanted to hide. There is still a very slight hint of her walk even to this day.

With these thoughts in mind, I will return to my daughter, who after this marathon surgery, still had a great deal of healing to do and at some point, her expandable implants needed injecting with saline. But not, I might add, using the DIY method.

15

How Much is that Doggy?

Diary extract, 8th June 2009:

Three days after the bilateral mastectomy, she is slowly recovering, I'm still staying in the parents' ward, but hopefully not for much longer. Ellen and I have hatched a plan to persuade her dad to say yes to having a dog; she has wanted one ever since her guinea pigs died. So, fingers crossed it will work! I still feel guilty over their demise!

It was a cold and dreary evening and, as always, I trudged outside to feed the guinea pigs and tuck them in for the night. Draping the old blanket over the cage, I turned and hurried back inside, keen to get out of the cold and onto the next task. It wasn't until the following morning that I realised I'd made a terrible mistake. Looking out of the window, I noticed what seemed to be a scattering of fur across the grass. I couldn't have forgotten to make sure the cage door was closed, could I? With my heart in my mouth, I rushed outside envisaging poor old Popsy, always the inquisitive one, being teased, torn apart and then dragged away to be enjoyed by one of the foxes that would often be seen creeping around the hutch. I was certain it was bad news for Popsy and as I peered into the cage, how relieved was I to see Honey still alive, cowering in the corner?

"I bet you can tell me what happened. It's lucky, that thankfully, you didn't follow Popsy out of the cage," I whispered softly to her, followed by a sigh of pure relief, that, thank goodness, her favourite had been saved.

Sadly, as guinea pigs are naturally sociable creatures, Honey didn't live much more than a couple of months. Her back legs gave out and then a day or two later she went to join Popsy, leaving Ellen without the companionship of a pet at a time when she needed one the most.

With both the guinea pigs and her chest gone, there was now a need, more than ever, to hatch a plan for another pet. Her attention was focused on something larger, and she was desperate for a dog. She pestered and beleaguered, and we had generally heard nothing else for many months. All a dog meant to me at that time was yet another being that would have to be looked after, cared for and fed, so if the truth be told I wasn't particularly keen. That is, until I saw her the morning after her surgery, looking like death personified. The only hurdle was her dad, who felt the demands of a dog would be too much. I looked down at my 13-year-old, drugged-up daughter, who was the same colour as her hospital sheets, thinking that no one would be able to refuse her anything, particularly now. Nobody, or nobody with a minuscule of compassion anyway.

"I know and I'm keen for you to get a dog and I think that the only way is to appeal to your dad's more sympathetic side."

I suggested to her that she asked him again, whilst she lay in her hospital bed, having undergone many hours of surgery, limp, pathetic and looking close to death; this I told her would play in her favour, and now was the time. If nothing else, using emotional manipulation; let's face it, that's what I was suggesting, to covertly influence her dad. It seemed a sensible ploy. Use all the ammunition you have.

Into the ward walked her dad followed by the boys. I casually moved off the bed to let him sit down next to her. He didn't say anything but gave her a kiss and held her hand. I developed a bit of a cough at that point and hoped she would understand this was code for go for it. That's when she said, right on cue, "Dad, please, I would really like a puppy, please can I have one?"

That's my girl, her very convincing, sad voice and a face that was whiter than white, she deserved at the very least a Golden Globe award. I took a deep breath, gave her a nod and a wink and hoped he would say all the right things. There was a fairly long pause and then he said a firm, "No", stood up and walked to the window. Sensing this wasn't the end of the matter, or at least not wanting to allow it to be, I thought I'd see how it played out before stepping in. Keep cool, keep composed and keep positive. He paused at the window, there was a slight hesitation before returning to her bed. Come on, come on don't keep her in suspense.

Then he whispered, "Ok."

Ellen was actually smiling. Alright then, a green light and it was all systems go. We had already been talking about different breeds; would we get a Bichon Frise, a Schnauzer, or how about a Westie? Whatever dog we went for had to fit into our lifestyle and be able to work around us.

Sitting with her in the children's ward, we trawled the internet looking for our perfect dog. She wanted it to be a girl, small and cuddly and it positively had to be black. Looking at lovely little puppy photos was a great distraction and we were able to while away the hours doing an activity that didn't involve boobs. It was truly a pleasure and something we looked forward to and took our minds off all that had happened, transporting our thoughts to a place of hope and a future without problems, well breast problems anyway.

After a few days, sitting on her bed in the ward, cooing and ahhing over so many gorgeous dogs, we found one - in Wales. This was too far for us to travel; we just didn't have the time. A leap of faith had to be made and after ringing the breeders, who asked me many questions about why we wanted a dog, without too much of a fuss, an endearing little cockapoo was sold to the girl on the children's ward. Strike while the iron is hot! The boys were so pleased and wanted to see a picture, it wasn't particularly clear and quite honestly, we just had to believe that the dog we had virtually bought unseen, was a happy, healthy pooch. Her dad couldn't quite believe we had moved so fast and I thought it unwise to mention the cost. What did it matter?

We arranged to have her delivered, unseen, on my daughter's

14th birthday, three weeks after her mastectomy and a week after leaving the hospital. Our gorgeous puppy was driven down in a van by the breeder. The arrival of this adorable little fluffball was like having a magic wand waved over our family. She entered our house in a whirlwind of scampering, whining and licking and we were instantly under her spell; smitten. After so many difficult and emotional periods in my young daughter's life, this little creature provided the comfort that even her family seemingly couldn't provide. The smile on her face was so worth it. I hadn't shared a smile like it for so very long. Whatever chaos and disruption this puppy may bring it was worth it to see the happiness on my daughter's face. Puppy cuddles can fix just about anything.

Our little puppy wormed her way into our family and all the rules that my husband had laid down as the law, about not letting her sit on the sofa, not going upstairs and not feeding her at the table all went out of the window. To this day, she can roam around the house, sit or sleep wherever she likes, go outside when it suits her and is fed the best of everything. It's a dog's life.

We felt that you should be shown this photo of a painting, which is of our lovely dog, at the grand old age of 12 years. It is so much nicer to look at than the other pictures I have shown you. We all love her absolutely and unreservedly.

16

'One Flew over the Cuckoo's Nest'

"And so, I wake in the morning
And I step outside
And I take a deep breath and I get real high
And I scream from the top of my lungs
"What's going on?"

Diary extract: 9th June 2009:

There are moments when even as a mother you really don't know the best way to deal with your child's situation or events that happen. Today was one of those moments. I think I lost all kinds of perspective and, if I'm honest, felt depressed by what happened today but on the other hand, it could be a culmination of so many events leading up to this. I do know that when I look in the mirror, which isn't very often, I have a perpetual frown and a tense look on my face.

I shrugged my shoulders and with a feeling of despair said, "I give in and I hand over responsibility. Sorry, but I am at a loss to know what more I can do so I think it's best to remove myself from the situation." The nurses just looked at me.

I can only remember specific days in the hospital immediately after the big 'M', one of those obviously, being our lovely puppy purchase. Most days, however, merged into a blurry haze of medical routine. Perhaps this was simply from the point of view of self-preservation combined with the fact that the majority of time spent on the ward wasn't a whole lotta fun. One incident, however, still sticks with me and probably will do forever.

Since having a rather large chunk taken off her chest, she was still very much in need of regular pain relief, so a strict timetable was put in place. That is until this inauspicious day. As the nurse administered the prescribed dose, I half-listened as she explained there'd be a slight change in the medication. Fair enough, there'd been so many drips and pills and prescriptions that it was hard to keep track and I thought as long as she wasn't feeling pain, it was fine by me. Except, suddenly and seemingly out of nowhere, my daughter, I kid you not, went berserk.

As Ellen describes it:

This pain relief meant that I wasn't in too much pain at all, but I do remember the drugs making me so high, no worries, concerns and just thinking about the now. I had a real urgency to know the name of a nurse who I liked and there wasn't really any rationale behind it. The nurse wasn't on duty but they did show me a picture of her! I had no concerns or worries about dragging everything behind me, up the ward and away from the nurses and Mum, although the drains did tug a little. I don't recall being taken back to bed, but I do remember feeling very tired afterwards as I hadn't done so much walking in a long time. I remember Dad coming in and being very quiet with me.

My description is a little different. From our side, it was like being part of a crazy hospital scene in a movie. She leapt off the bed, no mean feat when she was tethered by tubes and bags, legged it up the ward, yelling at the top of her voice. She shouted at me to go away, insisting that she wanted to get out and demanding to know the name of one particular nurse. She was adamant that it was this nurse – not even Nurse Upbeat – she absolutely needed to see and wouldn't take no for an answer. As it was, that nurse was off duty and was extremely sorry she hadn't been there to help. Lucky escape for her I'd suggest.

My itinerant daughter headed off down the ward, wired, upset and downright difficult to deal with, let alone to calm down. In the space of five minutes, she had turned into a yelling, screaming banshee with no regard for where she was or who was there. The nurses and I were shocked into action, and we ran down the ward after her and in voices that wouldn't wake up sleeping children, appealed to her to stop and cool down. Our words just fell on deaf ears. And those sleeping children were now wide-eyed and stunned into silence as they heard and then saw this rebellious patient, who to all intents and purposes may have been trying to escape.

We did our utmost to prevent her from rampaging all over the ward, with all and sundry dragged along in her wake. But this patient wasn't going to allow herself to be caught. She was completely unaware of the disruption and commotion that she was causing, and I had a fleeting vision of the other patients jumping out of bed, wielding their bedpans, pulling out their tubes and joining her in a breakout.

Right, that's it, enough is enough. There are moments in a mother's life when you simply can't be accountable and so I handed over this problem to the nurses "*And I step outside and I take a deep breath*," and went to sit in the car. Relinquishing my responsibilities? Yes, I was. Hiding? Sure, perhaps I felt I was within my rights though. After all, it wasn't me who'd decided to change her medication.

Ensconced in the car, I leaned my head back, closed my eyes and I tried very hard to calm down. My mind, however, kept replaying her tugging at the tubes and pipes that were attached to her body as she raced up the ward. It must have been painful, why didn't this stop her or even slow her down? How much damage could she have inflicted on herself?

A tap on the window brought me back to the present, it was her dad, who had come to visit her. Well, wasn't he in for a surprise? I poured out the whole dismal story. How much he believed or what he was expecting when he entered the ward, without me, was uncertain. No way was I going back in there just yet. I knew I had painted a rather bleak picture of madness and mayhem, but that's what happened. Anyway, I thought, his favourite film has always been 'One Flew Over the Cuckoo's Nest' and now he had the chance to take part in his very own version, with a very real possibility that the main character had already flown the nest.

By the time I plucked up enough courage to leave the safe haven of the car, she had calmed down and was, thankfully, looking and behaving normally, sitting back in bed with all the tubes and pipes in place. As I went to find the nurses, I heard her say to her dad that she knew she was behaving oddly but she had this strange feeling of being high and just wasn't able to stop. That's about right.

The nurses, looking a little ashen explained that she had come down to earth pretty soon after I had left and luckily there was no damage done to herself or anyone else. All the nurses were extremely apologetic, they'd never witnessed such a reaction. It wasn't anybody's fault, just an unfortunate set of circumstances. I did request – no, beg - that she wasn't given this same medication again. Not surprisingly, the nurses wholeheartedly agreed and had already put a big red cross against it. The plan, universally, was for the pain medication to be the same as before and they were under no circumstances to try anything new. I one hundred per cent agreed with that decision.

I was a bit careless, probably because I was still a little shell-shocked, but I didn't make a note of the name of this dastardly medication. We have, therefore, all just got to hope that she is never given it again or if for some awful reason she is, maybe in the future, she might not react again in the same way or if at all. Fingers crossed.

After the madness subsided and we all returned to our usual semblance of normality, I half-considered suggesting we spend the evening watching a movie. *One Flew over the Cuckoo's Nest* maybe? Maybe not.

17

Backside Over Breast

June 2009

Diary extract: June 18th:

Being the child or should I say teenager that she was, Ellen has been persistently picking and pulling at the plasters and tape, which are there, I continued to tell her, for a good reason, to help wound healing. I'm very afraid that if she continues it's not going to be a very pleasant result. I can foresee trouble ahead.

As she was sitting in a shallow bath, because getting the top half of her body wet was not an option, I caught her at it. "Stop it, leave your tape and plasters alone, stop picking. They are there for a reason, they must remain in place until everything has healed!"

She'd been home from the hospital for two weeks and it was so important that the healing process was allowed to take place. The way she was attacking her chest bandages, it was unlikely anything was going to heal.

"I'm just taking a look, no harm in that."

"Yes, there absolutely is." I could see that an incision underneath her left breast was definitely not looking good. "Ellen, leave it all alone, this area needs to be kept an eye on."

"Oh, it's fine."

It certainly wasn't fine, but I didn't say any more. I thought we'd just wait and see. Her body was pretty good at bouncing back relatively well after surgery. Panic not, at least not yet anyway.

Bath over and done with, plasters and tape back in place, she decided to make the most of the lovely morning and walk the dog into town. She'd set her sights on a purse from Kath Kidston, as a treat to herself and why not? This was the first time she had wanted to go out and I didn't mind, it was a 20-minute walk that she had done many times. She'd spent so many days incarcerated either in hospital or in her bedroom, feeling trapped within four walls. Fresh air, different surroundings and taking part in life again were very much needed. It also gave me a breathing space to change her bedsheets, cook dinner and do all the other mundane chores without having to be interrupted by requests for drinks and food. Delighted, I told her to take care, not to walk too far and to remember she was still convalescing. The problem was I had said these words all too often and they had become a bit meaningless. She gave a perfunctory nod and off she went.

Under normal circumstances, this should have been a risk-free activity, but this was not a normal situation. The removal of her two very large breasts, just two weeks ago, the dog still a puppy and not able to walk too far, a restriction on exercise and added to all this was the weather. It was a very hot June day. Put all this into the mix and you end up with a recipe for disaster. What was I thinking? By the time she returned home, it was late in the afternoon, and I was getting a little worried. She came into the house carrying the dog under one arm and shopping in the other, Oh wow!

"Glad to see you back, did you get your purse?" I said taking the dog from under her arm. I looked at my exhausted, white-faced daughter and I had to consider what the cost of this trip to the shops may mean. Avoiding weight-bearing exercises, strenuous lifting, staying cool and keeping dry, had been forgotten. It was too late to say anything that would in any way help the situation.

"I forgot the dog wouldn't be able to walk so far, being a puppy, so I had to carry her most of the way back. I also thought

I would go past the park and let her have fun."

I looked at the dog as she happily scampered out into the garden, without a care in the world and then I looked at my exhausted daughter as she collapsed into the nearest chair.

I knew I had overdone it and pushed myself too far, especially when I had to carry the dog because she just sat on the pavement and refused to move. We were both so hot and tired but because I felt as if I'd been locked up for weeks, I wanted to make the most of going out.

Was this the time to panic? There would be consequences I was certain. I was right. The inescapable result of this innocuous and simple activity was for the area that was already refusing to heal as quickly, to give up and not heal at all. I insisted that we check the area before she went to bed and although I had suspected a certain amount of distress to the area, I wasn't expecting what I saw; the tape that was covering some of the operated area was only just hanging on and underneath this was a vicious-looking open wound, which was bleeding green, fluorescent gunk. Holy Maloley! It resembled something you'd possibly find in a nuclear waste plant, and it was oozing from Ellen's body. Red alert, action needed to be taken.

I rang the children's ward that night. The next day, amidst her grumbling and moaning, we were off again to the same hospital she was in only two weeks ago. As a patient, Ellen, not surprisingly, was still uppermost in their minds and it was a pleasant surprise to see Nurse Upbeat. He gave her an immediate injection of antibiotics and cleaned and dressed the wound. This was all done with a sprinkling of jokes, teasing and good-humoured banter, especially when we told him what she had been doing the day before to cause this mess. He blamed the dog. Quite right too.

Unfortunately, the wound had become too large to heal on its own and she was told that it would be necessary to have a skin graft, which helps to heal the area quicker and reduces the risk of infection. Well, would you believe it? Yes, I absolutely would. I was aghast, and for Ellen, it was an unmitigated disaster. The only thing she wanted less than another stay in hospital was another operation. Sadly, sadly, there was just no other choice so, it was back to the ward once more. An absolute catastrophe. Her stay was only two days, but she was beyond listening to words of support or sympathy.

I did have thoughts of running away but I just couldn't work out how I would get through the limited openings in the windows of my room, wearing a hospital gown. It would look pretty suspicious running down the motorway but that was how I felt. This was the very last place I wanted to be. Anywhere but here.

The skin graft from her buttocks, which is the most common site to use, as it is usually hidden and cosmetically less important, was a success and the wound healed quickly. It was a surprise though that the patch on her backside was more painful than the one under her breast. Apparently, the donor site area is usually more painful than the grafted area because the top layers of the skin are removed, exposing the nerve endings. Luckily healing was her thing, and I was sure that it wouldn't be long before her backside felt normal again. In the end, though, it took almost three weeks before it felt anything like approaching normal.

"Right young lady, no fiddling with the bandages covering the wound, no carrying the dog, no long-distance walking and no strenuous exercise or weightlifting." Even though there was a bit of humour in what he said, it was clear Nurse Upbeat meant every word. I did think of adding my advice but thought better of it and remained quiet.

"Anything I CAN do?" Ellen asked sarcastically.

"No, not really except take care, we don't want to see you back here again."

She accepted what he said and for once it wasn't me laying down the law. This time she was told by the nurses that if she was to avoid coming back to hospital then this was how it had to be. Poor Ellen, I really felt for her and aside from very short walks with the dog to ease her claustrophobia, she stuck to the rules and as a result, healed nicely. And this was how she spent the summer of 2009.

Backside After Breast pictures. July 2009

First picture taken before going to the hospital – yuk!

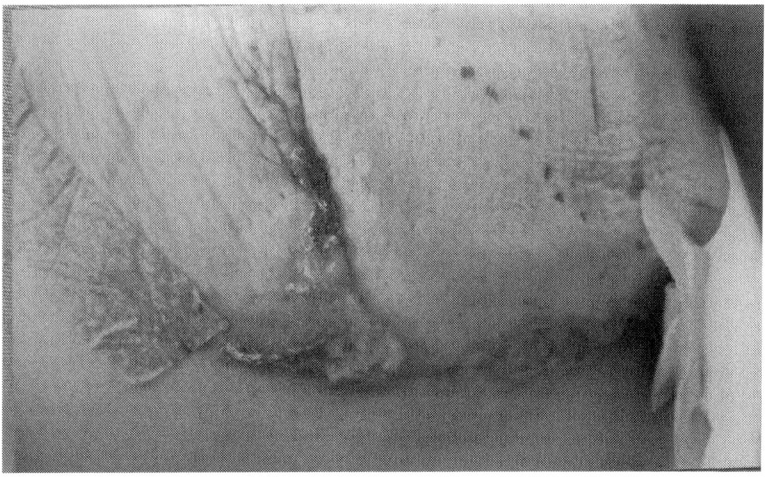

Hospital photographs before the skin graft:

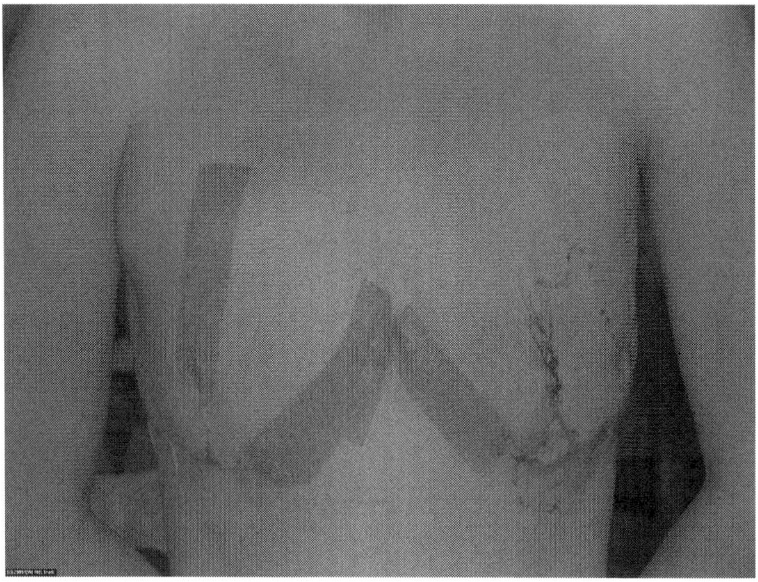

A picture of her backside the donor site! Photograph taken once she was home.

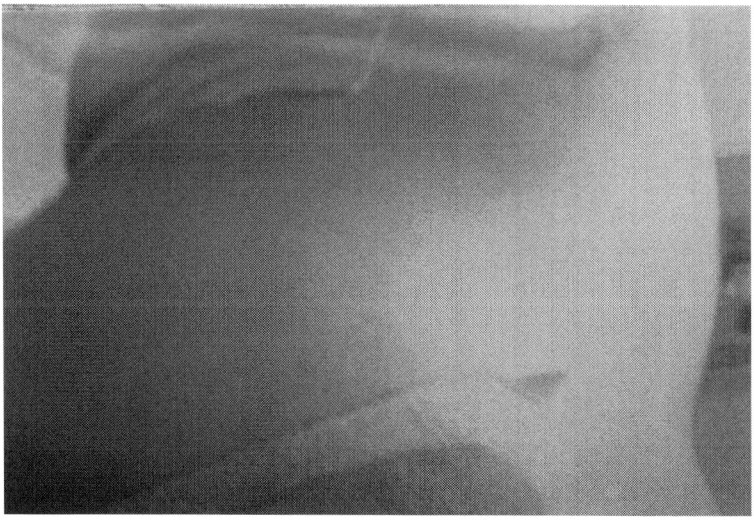

18

The Old School Yard

2000-2009

Remember the days of the old schoolyard,
we use to laugh a lot…
we used to cry a lot…

Cat Stevens, 1977

Obeying the rules was the only way Ellen's body was going to heal. She understood this and had the dread of ending up back in hospital to help keep her on the straight and narrow. However, not all rules are made equal. There are even some that seem made just to be broken. In all the research I've done on dyslexia the one thing that comes up time and again is that dyslexic pupils can put so much effort and energy into avoiding reading, writing, spelling and any other affected skills that it can be considered poor behaviour and a refusal to listen, when in reality it's avoidance tactics for something they find very difficult.

For the majority of us, our early life is defined by school. We all remember those days, the good and the bad. As time moves on and memories fade, only the key events, those which have caused us the most happiness or sadness, remain. Ellen's schooldays weren't always easy but that is not to say that she was constantly unhappy.

I enjoyed learning and liked to be organised. I had to work hard and it was difficult because our classes were often disrupted by the same kids in my year. Before I grew so big, I liked to take part in sport but when it became impossible to run or squeeze my oversized chest into a bib, I had to stop. Art was a favourite lesson of mine but the teacher wasn't the kindest and once again, it became awkward to wear art overalls.

There were two issues from which she had no respite, Dyslexia and Gigantomastia. Two very different disabilities and as far removed from one another as you could get. The first was unseen but forever present, particularly within her academic life, and the other was tangible and all-consuming.

Dyslexia is best described as a combination of abilities and difficulties which affect the learning process in one or more of reading, spelling, writing and sometimes numeracy. Other weaknesses can be the speed of processing, short-term memory, sequencing, auditory and/or visual perception, spoken language and motor skills. Some children, like my daughter, had very good creative skills while others can have strong oral skills but overall, there are strengths that need to be encouraged by teachers.

According to some studies, dyslexia can be hereditary and occurs despite normal intellectual ability and conventional teaching; it is independent of socioeconomic or language background. Classified as a daydreamer, my daughter didn't choose to drift off in class, it wasn't a conscious decision on her part. The harder she tried to follow instructions, the more lost she became until eventually she just gave up. Instructions, one at a time, must be given concisely and clearly otherwise it will be an information overload for the student. As she was usually quiet, she didn't affect the classroom environment and so the teachers tended to focus on aggressive and impulsive behaviour.

Often I would tell the kids around me to be quiet and then I would be told off for saying something in class by the teacher and picked on by the student. No win situation.

Things were different at home. I'd learnt from when she was very young to give her clear, slow instructions. This gave her the chance to process, to think about what she'd been asked and then put it into practice. Once we'd cracked this, life became much easier for us both. I understood she wasn't just being wilful or naughty, and she felt considerably less frustrated.

My daughter had private tutoring to support her studies from 2006 through to just before taking her GCSEs in 2010. This support was invaluable, and it is impossible to measure the extent to which it contributed to the results she gained at GCSEs and A Levels. She had gained results that considering all the problems she faced were pretty damn good. She was determined to do well and she did. Her difficulties resulted in my furthering my research in dyslexia and ultimately led me into teaching and supporting children with similar difficulties.

She will always be dyslexic as fundamentally there are brain differences that are wide-ranging; there are deviations between dyslexic and non-dyslexic people in the brain's structure and function. In a nutshell, I think it's fair to say that if Ellen had not been dyslexic, on a day-to-day basis her school life would have been less difficult. I also know that this applies to so many other children who struggle to access the curriculum because of this unseen difficulty.

And so, we move on to her other nemesis, without which there would be no story. I have already mentioned in no uncertain terms some of the problems that arose at school from the Gigantomastia but there was one incident in the autumn term of 2009, just after her mastectomy, which must be told to illustrate the stress and the relentless pressure of everything she'd been going through.

My summer of 2009 wasn't a lot of fun, I had a mastectomy in the June, a skin graft in the July and August was spent getting over it all. By September I was back at school but this time I was actually able to take part in sports, if I was careful. No more spending the afternoons, when everyone else was out doing sports, in the library.

It was the end of September and I arrived at school and was trying to squash my games/sports bag into my locker. It was impossible, the locker was too small and my bag too big. So, although I knew I shouldn't, I left it on the top of the locker, otherwise, I was going to be late. There was a yell from across the hall and a senior teacher was shouting at me to put it in my locker and not leave it on the top. I told him that it wouldn't fit but he just kept yelling at me to try.

"Put it in your locker and get to class."

"I can't, it won't fit."

"Put it in and go."

I realised then and there that I was finished. Crying, I flung the bag across the room and left, my locker door still open, with half of my stuff hanging out and home I went; it was only 9.15 in the morning and I couldn't tolerate anything anymore. I left everything behind but my phone and walked right out of school. I was really sobbing by now, but I was done, done with being told off, done with teachers who didn't care, done with so-called friends and done with just about everything.

I had no particular friends at school, as I no longer cared about tedious gossip, clothes and shopping and basically felt a lot older than my years. No one understood or was that interested in what had happened to me, they all had their own problems. No one really talked about it to me, not what happened, not about how I felt. It or I had become a taboo subject. Very few friends stuck around for the difficult stuff.

I carried on crying as I walked home and worried a bit about what Mum and Dad would say. The school tried to contact me, but I just hadn't got the energy to reply. It took me over two hours to reach home and I think I was sobbing all the way. By coincidence, my eldest brother was leaving College; all his lessons had finished, and he bumped into me. I walked home with him. He was surprised to see me especially as I told him I had walked all the way. He just listened to me as we walked the rest of the way home. I was very worried when Dad got home but he just hugged me while I sat on his lap and cried.

I did speak to the teacher concerned and asked what had made him shout at her and suggested that it would have been kinder to give her a hand or simply allow her to leave her bag on the top of the locker for the time being. Oh no, dear me, he couldn't do that. It would set a precedent, and everyone would be doing it. I asked why it was that she couldn't be allowed a little leniency considering everything. It was the same old story; it wouldn't have been good for her to be singled out for special dispensation. Just a little leniency and kindness would have gone a long way. Honest to God I was dealing with Neanderthals.

She had just one more year to go and as this was her GCSE year, a lot of that time would be spent studying at home. As much as she wasn't happy, she just needed to hang on in there. Resilience, determination and a positive mental attitude had so far got her through a stage in her life when her breasts were either too large or, like now, flat, and two major operations. It was important for her to draw on all her reserves to continue studying for GCSEs next summer, as well as take time out to rebuild her breasts. How many 14-year-olds can say that?

19

The Intervening Years

2009 - 2012

"Oh, oh ooh, ooh, uh-huh
Oh, oh ooh, ooh, uh-huh."

Diary extract: November 4th, 2009:

I truly wasn't looking forward to this third visit to the breast care nurses. Her expandable implants continued to need saline injected into them and this necessitated finding the port and sticking a needle into it. Ellen by now had had enough of pain and her threshold was zero. We were going to have more fun and games today, I'm certain of it.

"This is seriously hurting. Can't you get someone who can put the needle into the port accurately?"

She'd never been one for mixing her words, so the nurse duly went off to find someone who was a little more practised at finding the port and injecting the saline. With the skin graft out of the way she now had her tissue expanders to deal with. This meant regular visits to the hospital to have a small amount of saline injected into them through the ports. Important because her young skin would easily shrink back, and a space had to be made for when her permanent implants would replace them.

Ellen's skin was weak and fragile and the upshot of this was for her to find the procedure painful and when whoever had the pleasure of doing this found it difficult to pinpoint the port, a lot of prodding, poking and stabbing went on, a little like trying to thread cotton through the eye of a needle. With a great deal of moaning and groaning from her, the breast care nurse or the doctor, trying to be as careful as possible, would attempt to locate the port and then inject the saline.

This procedure was really cringey. The port was a little round button attached to a tube which was connected to the temporary implant. However, where it sat, was below my scars, which was over my ribs. So, every time they tried to find it, they would wiggle it about over my ribs, which felt very uncomfortable. I also wasn't a fan of the chit-chat that came with these appointments and the long 45-minute drive each way.

The positive outcome of these visits was that they gave her chest a normal shape and size. Once flat, it was now a more appropriate and better shape for a 15-year-old, although they wouldn't be complete breasts. The nipples and areola still had to be formed and this wasn't going to happen until her permanent implants were put in place. These would have to wait, one step at a time. Rome wasn't built in a day.

She not only had these visits but also consultant appointments, as well as resuming her sessions with the Arts Psychotherapist; her days without her two big breasts were busy, to say the least. She began her life at Sixth Form College with two blank domes, which under clothes gave her an acceptable look. She did have a few concerns about their shape and overall appearance but all in all, things were heading in the right direction. Her school life had been fraught with challenges and negative emotions, and I so very much wanted her to be able to move on and enjoy the coming years of A levels. She could have a clean slate and hopefully start afresh.

I did have a slight hesitation when she told me about the ski trip she wanted to sign up for at college. I wasn't convinced this was a good idea and all sorts of difficulties crossed my mind, but she was quick to point out that back in 2008, when she was in hospital, the boys had gone, so it was only fair that she should go now. Umm, tricky.

I know that skiing or snowboarding, either one is a lovely recreational winter sport, with clean Alpine air and beautiful, mesmerising scenery. The backdrop nearly always resembles a scene out of Narnia, with snow-covered trees and a frosty blue sky. It was a healthy, exhilarating sport but it was incredibly hazardous and could sometimes be extremely dangerous. This was certainly a conundrum, but was I able to refuse her? No.

So, she signed up and off she went. We dropped her off at the College, armed with a chest protector and every other protector I could find. When the decision had been made and I knew she was definitely going I looked online at the type of protectors that were available and ended up buying one for her chest, which was essential and knee protectors as she was snowboarding. There was, not surprisingly, a wide selection of safety equipment and for good reason. I could envisage many dangers lurking on this trip and sending her off with what in effect was body armour went towards making me feel that she would in some way be safe.

Waving her goodbye, I pushed to the back of my mind all the risks that accompanied snowboarding. Her life had been restricted so much that I just wasn't able to say that it was too risky, she shouldn't go. For sure it was risky, but I kept everything crossed. Watching her leave, I knew it was the right thing for her but the unease I felt didn't go until she came back at the end of the week, thankfully unscathed and having had a wonderful time. I was able to breathe a sigh of relief. No broken bones, no broken anything. Phew!

She was also able to buy clothes and bras that fit and made her look like the nearly sixteen-year-old girl that she was. This meant shaking off the previous feeling we both had of shopping blues and being able to happily visit all her favourite high street shops. It had been a long time since she was able to shop around and buy age-appropriate clothes. Whatever she chose, she was able to buy, safe in the knowledge that it would fit, not just for a month but for a lot longer and it was what she really wanted not what she had to make do with.

As for boyfriends, well I do know she had a small group of male and female friends, who were from school and had gone on to College together. They were simply friends and there were no romantic involvements. She did have one relationship after leaving College and going on to do an Art Foundation course. She was flattered by his attention and in some way surprised by the fact that he found her attractive. His reaction after she had made the decision to tell him briefly what she had gone through, was positive but the relationship ended when he went off travelling.

It wasn't until university that I found the confidence to form more permanent and worthwhile attachments, which weren't affected by the trauma of my past.

Understandably, she had a lack of confidence in her own body image and that affected how others saw her and how she behaved with other people. To be honest, it is only much later down the road or, 'up that hill', that she says she has more confidence in her appearance. She does add as a caveat that there are still times when she is aware of people staring and this makes her feel very exposed and self-conscious. I did say to her that I'm sure the stares are for very different reasons now. She is young, slim and pretty; I would suggest that these are good enough motives.

The plan to put permanent implants in was to wait until she had finished growing, around eighteen, which would also give her body a rest from being continually opened up and operated on and then closed up again. There's only so much of this that one young person and her family come to that, can bear. So, for the time being, it was plain sailing, and the situation was almost normal.

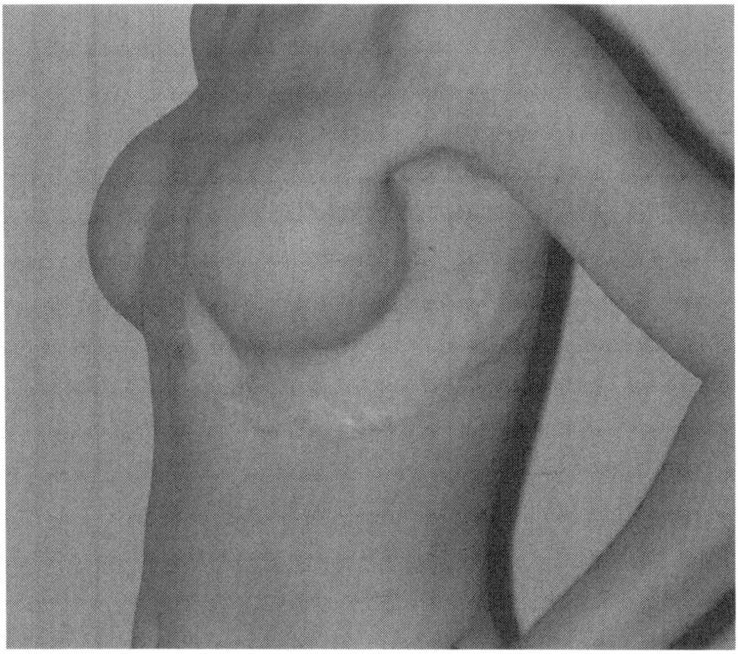

Hospital photo of the expandable implants, fully expanded.

20

Turkey or Bust

July 2012 – aged 17 years

A Saturday morning in July:

I woke up to a gloriously sunny day and one with nothing of significance happening. I had it all to myself, luxury. Perhaps I would potter around in the garden, sit in the sun reading a book, who knew I would simply take the day as it comes. This was a very optimistic attitude of mine, that as it turned out failed to materialise.

The Turkish coast is a beautiful and popular holiday destination. Ellen had arranged to go with a group of friends to stay in a villa close to the sea. Understandably, she was very much looking forward to this trip and I was pleased that this holiday, at last, would be stress-free, with no breast baggage and swimming costumes galore to choose from. How wrong could I have been?

"Mum, Mum, help, it's gone down, it's burst," she yelled from her bedroom, while simultaneously sobbing.

"What on earth has happened?" I shouted.

"Oh, I can't believe it!"

"I'm on my way, just hang on."

The panic in her voice made me drop what I was doing immediately. Taking the stairs two at a time, I found her in her room, topless in front of the mirror, staring at her breasts in shock and dismay. Ah, I knew right away what had gone down and what she couldn't believe. Somehow, not quite sure how her left breast was as flat as a pancake. I was momentarily surprised and lost for words; my brain was groping around for the right expression of sympathy and support. I completely failed, I opened my mouth and said,

"It might not be as bad as you think!" Duh, what was I thinking?

"Mum, it's flat, how can that be better than I think? I go on holiday next week and where've all the insides gone?"

"You're right and I don't know but we'll get it sorted." The old familiar sinking feeling, pin-sticking and thoughts of 'what now?' came flooding back. She's had two or three fairly normal years and we had been lulled into a false sense of security.

So, what exactly had happened? A while back, she had swapped the energy healer for yoga classes. Although both were good for the mind and soul, it would seem not to be the case for certain parts of the body. This particular morning she'd been doing her best to perfect the bow pose; backbend stretch for the whole front of the body, especially the chest. She said that at the time she felt that the implant had changed but wasn't sure in what way. As soon as she got home, it soon became obvious what had happened, the left implant had ruptured, its saline contents leaked out and the implant deflated. Well, would you Adam and Eve it?

The right side was still intact, was this a good thing? I couldn't quite decide. To have one up and one down wasn't exactly the look she was going for.

"Perhaps," I said to her trying to find a bit of humour in all this, "that pose ought to carry a health warning to all women with expandable implants?"

"Just not funny."

"Could be a good title for a name of a song, or band, 'Yoga and the Implants'?" I knew, at this point, I was on very dodgy ground.

This momentary lapse into frivolity had given me a chance to think a little and I realised that these expandable implants are only for short-term purposes and yet these had been in place for almost three years. In short, they were way beyond their sell-by date. The recommendation was for her to have the final implants done at around eighteen years old. Giving her body and psyche a long rest was vital before embarking on yet another operation.

This incident, however, was surely going to hurry this procedure along. An alternative was to deflate the right implant, but this was unlikely as I knew that it was essential to keep the skin stretched. Once deflated, the skin would most likely shrink back, making the insertion of permanent implants difficult. My other consideration was what had happened to the contents of the implants and what other damage if any, might have been done. With all these possibilities whirring around my mind, and yet another sinking heart, I do wonder how much sinking my heart can take, I contacted the hospital where she had had all her operations.

Instructed to go to the Minor Injuries Unit, we drove into the car park, and no sooner did we see the familiar collection of buildings than we too became very deflated. The hospital staff had done an amazing job, but it was the emotional links attached to it that by entering the premises had brought it all flooding back. The smell of the place, we thought we had buried, brought an unwelcome reminder of all the sadness and past events. Even so, I kind of grinned to myself, thinking that every time we came here it was either to increase or decrease her breast, a continual series of ups and downs. This visit was different though because it was only one breast that was up and the other one was down. That's a variation of the facts. I allowed myself a wry smile.

Gathering our emotions, we sat down in reception. Thankfully, we didn't have to wait too long for a very nice, young and smiling doctor to show us into his room. As always it is beholden to the patient, or patient's mother, to be a walking encyclopaedia on the whys and wherefores of their illness, treatment and the operations that had been carried out as he obviously knew nothing about her situation. I was pretty sure he hadn't got time for the full-blown explanation of the last six years, so he was given a brief, potted version from us both and after a quick examination, he confirmed that her left tissue expander had most certainly deflated, the consequence of which had left her with severely baggy skin where the expandable implant had been. It looked very much like wrinkly, sagging skin in old people. There she was with a crumpled and wrinkled chest on one half, and the other half remained the shape of a boob. Seriously, you couldn't make this story up, if you tried, it was just too bizarre and dare I say it, all too predictable, based on experience. We had gone for so long without a problem, I guess whoever or whatever has the blueprint of our lives felt it was now time to shake it up and give us a kick up the backside. Thanks!

The doctor put our minds at rest and assured us that the solution in her implants was only saline, which we knew already, but it was good to get it confirmed, and this would have been absorbed by the body. He was encouraging about the holiday and said that if she wanted to go, then by all means do so.

Great, that was good for us both, then he asked where she was going and it was at this point it all became a little tricky. She explained that they were staying in a Turkish villa, he looked horrified and told her, quite seriously, not to travel to Turkey. My first, very confused, thought was that Turkey must surely be a bad destination for someone with only one breast: Er that honestly can't be right.

It soon became clear why he had reacted as he did, as he was of Greek nationality, Turkey was the very last place he would have gone. My mind and certainly not Ellen's, however, was not concentrating on the history of relations and mutual hostility between Greece and Turkey. He did give a weak smile, though, put his grievances and bias aside and told her to have a lovely holiday. That was all she wanted to hear, apart from maybe being given a second breast to go on holiday with. That would have been a bonus.

I was still a little concerned about how she would feel going away with a mixed, male and female, group of friends and this rather strange physical situation she found herself in; that is her chest being half up and half down. I was pretty sure that if it had been me, I would have decided against putting myself into a position that would most likely have caused me embarrassment. I wasn't, however, going to influence her either way, not now I knew there was no danger. Selfishly, I would have preferred her to stay and not go but it wasn't my choice to make. Ellen was adamant that the holiday was still going ahead and seemingly unconcerned. I dropped her off, two days later, at the airport.

This time around she was minus any chest, knee protectors and general body armour, that she had taken skiing, but I did suggest she take breast inserts just for the side that was no longer there. Had she thought of this? Affirmative, of course, she had, and she had already sorted out something that could be used as stuffing and padding. Apparently, there is a plethora of methods on the market to choose from when thinking about stuffing your bra. Who knew it was a big business? Choices abound, the sock method, falsies or chicken fillets, which are typically made of silicone and are shaped like half-moon boobs; the tissue method and the double bra method, to name just a few so take your pick.

It was obviously, up to her how she dealt with this tricky situation. I wasn't going to be with her and although I would help her in any way I could, the problem was hers and hers alone. My daughter's preferred method of bra stuffing was to use the sock method. Yes, cheap, easy and always available. This is what she had to say:

I finally had a group of friends that I could go away with, and nothing was going to stop me from going. I stuffed my strapless bandeau bikini with socks and just hoped that no one really saw or cared, I just wanted a holiday. At seventeen this was the best I had felt. I was super brave at a water park where we all went on banana boats; a speed boat pulls you along and everyone gets thrown off into the middle of the ocean. I was seriously worried about everything falling out – but equally this was hilariously liberating.

What she had experienced, over the last six years, all the pain and suffering both mentally and physically had been immense. I can only think that these experiences had given her inner resolve and strength. She was a fascinating combination of vulnerability and resilience, and I would defy any adult to deal with it as well as she did. The holiday was going ahead whether she had one, two or no breasts. Good for her.

21

The Real Deal

Bilateral Exchange of Beckers Expandable Breast Implants for Fixed Volume Implants

Diary extract, Friday 30th November, 2012:

This is the day she is having her permanent implants put in. No more growth of breast tissue and no more breast deflation, hopefully! Not sure how I feel about her having another operation, but it isn't ideal for her to have the odd shape that she is now. So, it must be, most definitely, the best way forward. I'm hoping there will be no surprises lurking around the corner.

Her main man, Mr Charmingly-Direct saw her in September, around two months after the deflation, during which time Ellen had become fairly adept at bra stuffing and coping with yet another abnormal situation, the plus side being she was in control this time. We visited him in a different hospital than the one we had originally gone to for our very first Plastic Surgeon consultation, which was set in the lovely location. It didn't have the comfortable surroundings or the quiet feeling of calm but to be honest, these factors weren't of great importance this time around. We hoped that this meeting would ensure that the operation would follow swiftly. He was, as usual, sympathetic and understanding about her situation, there were also a few jokes from us all about her circumstances. It's always important to be able to laugh, no matter what. During the appointment, he explained to us,

"You need to be aware of the potential issues with scarring, capsular contracture long term and indeed a further need for implants. You also need to be aware of the limitations of surgery, especially because of her original problem and the position and extent of the scars and the body frame."

It was just the two of us sitting at his desk in the consultation room and I'm pretty sure we just sat staring at him, looking a tad confused. What issues with scarring? What is capsular contracture and why will the operation have its limitations? Should I be taking notes on all that he was saying? I was certain I wouldn't remember. He explained it to us again using a little less technical jargon and as usual, he didn't beat about the bush or mince his words. He had been our constant through thick and thin, effectively holding our hands through the whole process. He was our hero but did he really have to tell us in no uncertain terms, the further risks that were involved in replacing these expandable implants with fixed-volume implants? I suppose the answer is yes, he did.

If I have learned anything about being a patient or a young patient's mother, it is this: it is important to remember what is being said to you and to ask questions if you haven't understood; it is helpful to get second opinions and it is also important to know, not that you necessarily want to, what could go wrong. Being forewarned is forearmed.

He continued to tell us that these new implants have an outer silicone shell and once inserted are filled with a fixed volume of sterile water. Unlike her expandable implants, these cannot be adjusted after the operation. That was fair enough, keeping them the same size was so much more preferable than dealing with a bust size that kept changing.

The sudden rupture of implants hadn't been that long ago and was still uppermost in my mind, so I had to ask what was the likelihood of this happening? He patiently explained that should a saline implant rupture, the salt water would be absorbed by the body and there would be a noticeable loss of fullness. Yep, we knew all about that. However, a silicone rupture is known as a 'silent rupture' because the gel tends to be contained in the scar tissue capsule the body forms around the implant. As a result, the rupture is only detectable via an MRI scan. Upon hearing this, I thought saline won the implant competition hands down.

Breast implants do not last a lifetime and will require a replacement at some time in the future. We were told that it is recommended they are replaced every ten years, which was not something we wanted to think about now. However, the good news was that implants are improving, and the implants today would be inferior to the ones in twenty years. Yes, this was certainly a silver lining.

There was another option. As she got older and carried more weight, she could opt for a fat transfer to the breast. This procedure eliminated the need for foreign implant materials and instead enabled unwanted fat from other areas of the body to be transferred to the breast, creating a more natural-looking outcome. This sounded like an excellent proposition to me.

This time around she was too old to be admitted to the children's ward, which left her feeling a bit sad. It had been a place that had seen her through an awful lot, where the nurses had almost become friends. Quite by coincidence, the smiley-faced, cheeky-chappie, Nurse Upbeat had seen us as we came into the hospital, and he made a point of coming to see her before the operation. This time, he did not do his usual smiley faces on her knees. I suppose now she wasn't in the children's ward, he perhaps thought she wouldn't appreciate his artistry. It was so nice to see him again especially as he had been in on it from the beginning. He told us more stories of his son, who he was very proud of, and how every weekend he would take him to play football. I know that Ellen wasn't necessarily interested in football but the fact that he took time out, yet again, to chat with her made all the difference. I think he supported Chelsea, which was a pity according to my husband because otherwise, he'd have been perfect. I hope I've got that right and not put my foot in it.

Ahead of the operation, she was asked how big and what size did she want the implants? To her and considering all that she had gone through this was a question she found hard to answer. It was a standard and important question for most women, but she had simply been so big for so long at such a young age:

I felt it was such an awkward question to answer, I didn't have any idea or reference to go on. As I never really had a chance to recognise my breasts at a size I liked. I'd never been a 'normal' size at all, so I didn't know what this looked like. What size should someone my size and age be? I needed help with this one. It was also quite an intense operation as it would be the final one – exciting, as it was, it was also quite emotional as it was now the end of a massive period in my life that had defined me for so long.

The decision was to go with the cup size D, reminiscent of her 'cute boobs'. This operation was a standard procedure and didn't involve anything out of the ordinary and thankfully it went smoothly and with no hitches. It didn't take long and she was back in the ward within three hours. All I can say is that this implant exchange surgery was a walk in the park compared to the big mommas of her operation world, the big 'R' reduction and the big 'M' mastectomy.

She was back home after only two days. The pain was most severe in the first few days, and there was quite a bit of swelling and a feeling of stretching over the breast which gradually subsided. The stitches were removed around a week later and after six weeks there was no pain at all and she was left with permanent, almost perfect size D breasts, minus the nipples and the areola.

She does remember when the binder and bandages were removed, a feeling of sadness, recollecting that her cute, natural, boob-size breasts, from 2008, with nipples intact, well one at least, were no longer there. All she had to show from this SIX-year ordeal was an empty canvas; two blank domes, filled with saline and so very far removed from her cute D-cups and going further back her itsy-bitsy, teeny, weeny polka dot bra she wore in the very beginning.

The unveiling of these was a bigger deal than all the other ops because it was final and permanent whereas all the others were temporary mock-ups. I felt really deflated as the reality of all the operations had ultimately resulted in 'silicone breasts, which I had never asked for in the first place and a hard thing to come to terms with without really understanding that these were to be the final result. Plus having real, normal breasts was an all too distant memory and this felt like the real tragedy as nothing more was to be changed and to me, they didn't resemble real breasts.

As I have said before if I could have stopped this all from happening, or could have taken on the problem myself I would have done it a hundred times over. With these very sad thoughts and Ellen's words ringing in my head, I convinced myself that it was even more essential to continue with what had been started and create the perfect breasts, or as near perfect as possible. I felt that this was so important for her to have breasts that were the right size and, even better, looked like normal breasts. For far, far too long and in fact in reality they had never been normal. She deserved normal breasts.

It was therefore my aim, that once the implants were in and in order to transform these two blank domes and create real breasts, to highlight the importance of having the nipples formed and then tattooed, as well as having the areola tattooed. This was all to be accomplished in the coming months and was in some small way a positive step in creating real-looking, normal breasts, which up to now had never seemed possible.

During her 'A' Level year it was necessary for her to continue having check-ups, whilst at the same time visiting the hospital to complete the final part of the cosmetic procedure. Her life, as a seventeen-year-old, could settle down and continue unhindered once more but this time in complete confidence that very little was likely to go wrong.

22

Tit for Tat

Areola Tattoos – A Meaningful Form of Ink

Diary extract, November 27th, 2013:

I know she's had enough of all the hospital appointments, and I absolutely understand. The thing is that it's really important for her to have this appointment for tattooing. If she doesn't, they'll look like blank domes forever more. I keep telling her that she is so close to completing the cosmetic work, just a few more visits. I'm very afraid, for her sake, that she'll stop. In other words, she's completely disconnected from her body. Her condition might be under control but the damage is permanent, in more ways than one. Which is so sad.

"I really don't want to be here, I don't care whether they get done or not, I'm over it, why recreate something that can't be recreated? Why put a cherry on a smashed-up cake, embellishing something that's just not worth embellishing?"

"But it is worth doing. I understand that you don't want more work done but having tattooing will complete the whole effect. They're an essential part of your reconstruction, if you like, they're the finishing touches."

"I'm so done with it all."

"This is the next stage, come on, not much longer."

Desperately I tried to encourage her and to use her analogy, I said they were the icing on the cake and a cake that certainly wasn't smashed up. I was having real trouble trying to make her believe this. To her, these finishing touches were bogus. She had nothing but negative feelings towards her breasts and how she considered their aesthetic appearance. They weren't the 'cute boobs' she had before and she was finding it very hard to come to terms with what she had been given; an empty breast canvas, which felt and appeared too firm and, in her eyes, not like real boobs at all.

I persevered trying to make her see that these small cosmetic operations were an important part of the final rebuilding of her chest. I pointed out that even though she may not feel like having it done now, later she'd be grateful for the formed nipples and areola on otherwise blank domes.

Back in June 2013, she had gone into the Day Surgery Unit to have a bilateral nipple construction and some scar revision. The Surgeon used skin from the area of the formed breast, where the nipples would have been located, to surgically create two new nipples. There were no problems when she had this done and she was in and out within a day. This was such an important part of the reconstruction process as it gave her a good cosmetic outcome, providing both breasts with a look that was as close as could be to authentic-looking boobs, looking more breast-like but, as yet, without the formation of the areola. So far so good, getting ever closer to the end product.

As usual, though, she was warned - more warnings, oh how we love them - that a reconstructed nipple wouldn't look exactly like or feel like her original nipple.

This was no surprise to me, as I had minimal to no sensation. Nothing was normal.

This is where I had to step in on her behalf: even though she was now eighteen years old and more than capable of explaining herself. I felt it was important for me to make it clear that, for obvious reasons, she had never had an understanding of what a nipple should look, feel or behave like. At eleven years old when her breasts started to grow, this fact was lost along the way, tangled up in the horror story that was her breasts; the devastating truth is that in reality, she was far too young to remember or to appreciate her breasts back when she wore her itsy-bitsy teeny weenie polka dot bra. She did not have a memory, understanding or experience of knowing what her nipples or areola should look or feel like.

I'm sure some would say that what you have never had you can't miss, but I think that this is a rubbish proverb. In her case, because she hadn't had the experience, she couldn't know the importance of what she was missing. I felt that it was vital for her, in years to come and looking into the future, that all the cosmetic surgery was completed, and her breasts were formed correctly. We had several disagreements over this issue. I knew she just didn't want to have to continue more hospital appointments which would mean more time away from her life but in the end, we came to a stalemate and the only way forward for us both was to compromise.

In November, therefore, which was several months after the nipple reconstruction and a major milestone towards perfection, it was necessary for her to see the Breast Reconstruction Nurse Specialist to begin the tattooing process. The nipples were to be tattooed to add colour and further tattooing was to create the areola. Nipple tattoos are real tattoos applied with needles that insert semi-permanent pigment into the skin. As it was semi-permanent, they explained, this would mean that the colour would fade and so three or four appointments would be needed as well as a 'top-up' every year. I wasn't certain, upon hearing this, that Ellen would agree to it but I just had to keep the faith and fingers crossed.

At the start of the tattooing, she was shown a selection of areola sizes and a variety of different colours, and she had to choose the most appropriate for her size and skin colour. It was a work of art. Now, as we both looked at the veritable array of colours, shapes and sizes, even I was at a loss to know which I would choose. As an eighteen-year-old girl who had never really known what proper nipples and areolas were, it was difficult for her to make an informed decision. I had trouble getting her to this appointment so asking her to choose an appropriate size and shape wasn't going to go down very well. When it was obvious that my daughter was not able, or simply didn't want to suggest any, the breast care nurse took charge. Help was very much needed, phew!

She remembers the pain being patchy. A topical anaesthetic cream was used to numb the area and this helped. Also, the nerve endings where the areola was to be tattooed had been damaged, causing the pain from the needles to be very random. I was surprised to find that each pinprick drew a minuscule amount of blood, which I suppose should have been obvious when the procedure involved skin being punctured by a very fine needle. Her breast may have been artificial, but her skin was still behaving as it should.

In this first session of tattooing, the areola was shaped and coloured a very pale pink. It was a great success and made such a difference, I made perhaps too much of a fuss about how this procedure had improved the look of her breasts. She accepted this fact reluctantly but I truly meant it. She returned for one final session to help deepen the colour, but this was unfortunately to be her last session. She had made up her mind not to continue; this was the compromise we had come to. Even though it was not my choice, I had to respect her decision.

To date, she hasn't returned to top up her colour, which I think is a shame. She had come so very far and all that was needed were a few more visits to the tattooist. Long gone were the days when I had to make the decisions for her and so for me, although I disagreed, it was also kind of liberating. I no longer had the responsibility. Ellen was at the age where she could make those choices for herself. That said, old habits die hard and even though we made a mutual decision to agree to disagree, I still might drop it into the conversation at some point in the future. My children always tell me I just can't let go.

By this stage, the hill she had climbed so far had become unendurable. She had begun to feel underwhelmed, to say the least, with anything to do with her breasts. She had had enough.

The hospital photographs after her breasts had been saline injected to the correct amount, back in 2009, were the last ones she wanted to be taken. From here on in there are no more photographs showing the real, fully formed and almost completed breasts; how they looked mattered not to her anymore and she cared even less. It may seem sad but it meant that getting on with her life was more important than obsessing about how her breasts looked and they looked a million times better than they had ever done in her whole life; except for her small budding breasts before all this began. It had only taken seven years to reach this point.

23

Just When You Think It's All Over

2016

A And I say, "Hey-ey-ey-ey"
Hey-ey-ey
I said, "Hey, what's going on?"

Diary extract, 20th May:

Well you go to bed one day, comfortably in the knowledge that all is well with your world and then bam, it's not! It was unbelievable that another little lump had begun to form and yet here we were, going back again to a hospital where we had had many lumps removed, only to have another one taken away.

"Do you want to know something funny?"

"What?"

"I've got a little lump that's been growing very gradually, and I think maybe it should be looked at. It has become bigger and weirdly seems to become sore around the time of my periods."

We were now so far up that hill that I suppose you could say we had all become a little blasé and allowed ourselves to breathe once more. Isn't it always the way, though, just when you think it's safe to move on something small and unwanted rears its ugly head?

I took a close inspection of it and in some strange way, it was quite sweet. You have to remember that we were all used to colossal-sized lumps, not a tiny miniature version. This sensitive little lump, in her right lower chest, was a mere baby at 3cm in diameter and was painful with her menstrual cycle. She complained of it being very tender to the touch and the fact that it was at the front, bottom right of her breast, made it uncomfortable and annoying. Any garment that fitted snugly to her chest would be restricted by this lump and become very irritating.

Quite obviously, her body was having another go and fighting back. I could almost hear it say: 'Don't think I'm giving in lightly. Just because you've had permanent implants put in and life is pretty much on track, I can still hit where it hurts.' I know I talk about her chest as if it was a separate, thinking entity but when you have seen tissue just continuing to grow as it had, it wasn't difficult to wonder whether her breast tissue had a mind of its own and maybe a voice. Strange but true.

Well, this was a goddamn turn-up for the books. Here we were, four years on from having her permanent implants and eight years from her mastectomy. Was it possible for this to be happening again? The universe's sense of humour had not gone unnoticed but I'm afraid it was impossible to laugh this one off. I know for sure that Ellen felt the same way. My eyelid was beginning to twitch, more heart sinking and pin stabbing, more eye-raising, and I immediately reverted to the let's get this sorted and dealt with mode. Right then, bring it on, here we go again. Except this time, we were off to visit the Rapid Access clinic, somewhere we'd never been before. A new place for a new problem. No more reminders, no more old memories.

We were sitting in the waiting room amongst many other women and as I looked around, it occurred to me that perhaps my daughter was by far the youngest and, more likely than not, the only one there who had had a mastectomy. I had to remind myself that it wasn't cancer and nor was it life-threatening which, unfortunately, may not be true for some of these women who were sitting with us in the room. Did this fact make what had happened up to now, any less traumatic and raw? I'm afraid not. There was, I thought, also that proverbial silver lining; the one advantage of my daughter's mastectomy would be never having to experience her boobs being squashed like pancakes during a mammogram. As long as there was no breast tissue left, please let that be true, mammograms would not be needed.

When I say, we had never been to this clinic before, we hadn't. But I had. I began telling my story to my daughter, anything to pass the time, while we waited. I explained to her that I had come for my usual mammogram, which provides X-ray images of the breast that can reveal early signs of cancer. My breasts were squished and squashed into the equipment.

"It's really uncomfortable and unpleasant, so there's your silver lining," I told her as I continued with the story.

The results of my being pummelled and prodded weren't as good as they could have been. Apparently, my right breast was showing some unusual tissue. UNUSUAL TISSUE. Oh, hello, and would you like to know about some *really* rogue tissue?

I think I choked on this information, more from the fact that I was pretty sure they had no idea, like I had, about unusual tissue. I could tell them a thing or two.

Once this information had been imparted to me in a very sensitive way, I was gently placed in a quiet room to digest this quite unbelievable news and a biopsy was arranged. I remember thinking, 'I'm certain I don't have breast cancer, this must all be a mistake.' The funny thing was, I really was so sure that there was no problem. In fact, the poor nurse who broke the news to me must have wondered why I had nearly broken into a laugh when she told me. I was obviously a slightly unstable patient that would have to be handled with kid gloves.

I waited in this pleasant room all on my own and thought about how they were wrong. Eventually, a nurse came and explained that I was to be taken to have the tissue examined and have a biopsy. Ok, I said fair enough. Into the room I went and lay down on the bed, top half off and thought about all those times that this had happened to my daughter when she was still so young. The nurse and I chatted until in came a fairly elderly gentleman who introduced himself and said that he would be taking the biopsy. My only thought was that I hoped he had a steady hand!

The biopsy needle was to be put into the right breast to remove what they considered to be the unusual tissue. He was very kind, but the needle was no walk in the park. I silently profusely apologised to my daughter for not being more sympathetic to her over the pain she went through. He explained that after removing the tissue for examination, he would be putting a little marker inside my breast that would identify the biopsy site to make it easier if, at a later date, they needed to go into the breast and remove this tissue. My brain was ticking away, whilst trying to ignore the pain in my right boob.

"So, what happens to this teeny, tiny marker?" I asked.

"Oh, it is simply removed at the same time as the breast tissue." He quipped adding that it didn't do any harm.

"Well, then what happens if my breast tissue is alright, what then, will I have to have it removed?"

"It remains in situ indefinitely, doing no harm."

I began to feel quite angry and indignant; nobody had told me that it would remain forever, snuggled up inside my breast.

In my nicest, calmest voice, I said, "Sorry, sorry I am not having a foreign body left in my right breast, to upset the status quo, absolutely no, no way." I was really rockin' with indignation. I was amazed that he considered it to be something so ordinary and natural to leave a foreign body inside my breast. No way!

Grandad, as I had decided to call him, was still poking and stabbing but the nurse was on my side and said it was my own choice. I wasn't so sure with Grandad, he continued, without saying a word. I could also feel sticky, warm stuff dribbling down my breast and later on after the biopsy had been taken and the offending disc removed from the room, she said he had looked quite upset. Mind you, when I saw the state of my right boob after his attack, I was upset too, it went from red through to purple and looked horrific. I spent the whole summer watching it change colour, becoming a summery yellow before turning to an autumnal brown. All because I didn't want to have a teeny tiny bit of metal inside me; surely my body, my choice.

Ellen thought this was hilarious and pointed out that it still wasn't anywhere near as bad as her stories. I agreed but I said my story wasn't done. As well as the biopsy I also had to go for an MRI scan. Despite knowing that I wasn't setting a very good example of good patient behaviour for my daughter, I continued my story. I hate confined spaces and I was terrified of being enclosed in what looked like to me a tin drum, especially while it banged, rattled and thumped. I tried to explain to the radiographer that I didn't want to do this, and did she mind?

"Well, it's in your best interests and there's really nothing to it," she calmly told me.

"Look, I don't want to waste your time, I'll just hop off the bed and let you see someone else," I said whilst thinking about my 89-year-old mother who was sitting waiting for me and who had in her day, been a radiographer. How could I tell her I'd wimped out?

I crumbled and gave in and close to tears, I put on the proffered headphones to listen to music that would drown out the noises. Eyes squeezed tightly closed, I prayed.

"Wow mum, just checking you've remembered what I had to go through - seen my chest lately?"

"I know, I know you were, and are, so much better at it than me. You did have lots of practice though!" I told her, as I gave her arm a quick squeeze.

The results of all this upheaval were, I'm pleased to say, cancer free, and I just had unusual tissue. Does this mean that I have been the one to blame, all along? I must apologise to my daughter but hang on a minute, what about my mum? I was about to tell her this last thought when a nurse came into the waiting room and my daughter's name was called out; we were on the march.

During this appointment, she had several tests, one of which was an ultrasound which revealed that the lump was accessory breast tissue with changes similar to the previous Gigantomastia. It was considered, medically, as not completely unexpected. In other words, it was a nasty little specimen of breast tissue which had been left behind after her mastectomy in 2009. The correct medical terminology is angiolipoma.

So here we have it, the crux of this disease, Juvenile Gigantomastia. The ever-growing breast tissue, the amount of tissue that had to be evacuated during the mastectomy was enormous, not even taking into consideration the amount of tissue taken away during the reduction. We had been told that it was essential, absolutely essential, that all the breast tissue was removed during the mastectomy so that there would be no more growth. This little baby, unfortunately, was the result of a small amount of breast tissue being left behind. Well, why does no one listen to me, it goes back to what I have said previously, that the larger her size, the more difficult the surgery and therefore in all probability, doesn't it stand to reason, that it must have compromised the removal of all the tissue? That's my theory anyway, whether it's right or wrong, I'm sticking to it.

In other words, any poor, young, unsuspecting female with Juvenile Gigantomastia must be seen sooner rather than later, before their size compromises the outcome. Too big is, without doubt, simply too big with regards to the operation and to the girl who is having to struggle with the psychological and physical effects. This may have been a small lump but it was no less worrying and surprises like this one were a little difficult to bear. Were there going to be any more because we were all done with them? How can we be sure that this won't happen again? We just had to keep the faith and assume, that after the removal of this little lump, all the tissue would have finally and irrevocably been removed.

Mr Charmingly-Direct in his own inimitable way, explained in detail that this lump could be accessed via her old scars and then went on, as usual, highlighting all the difficulties; there will be pain, discomfort, potential wound problems, bleeding and infection. Love him!

There was, amazingly, a plus side to the excision of this lump and that was the chance to carry out some corrective, cosmetic surgery at the same time in the area where the tennis ball had been. Just goes to show that if you look hard enough there is always a silver lining.

She was back in the hospital that she knew all too well in May 2016 and the various operations were carried out. She had a pure graft fat transfer, from her thigh to the area where the tennis ball had been removed, this was to help rebuild and fill in the indentation it had caused underneath her armpit. It is a surgical process by which fat is transferred from one area, this happened to be her thigh, to the area under her armpit. The surgical goal is to improve or augment the area where the fat has been injected.

Unfortunately, the fat transfer wasn't a huge success. She didn't feel that the indentation had really been corrected and the area on the inside of her thigh was pretty painful, so all in all, the pain was not worth the outcome of the operation. This is still an ongoing area of concern for her. Also, she had what they called 'dog ear' which put simply was an unattractive fold between her breasts and is a term which refers medically to excess skin and fat that 'puckers' out at the incision lines. In Ellen's case, it developed at the point where the incisions came together near the centre of the chest, in a position where natural breasts have a cleavage. This was removed without a hitch and her chest was all the better for its removal, although it still didn't give her a natural cleavage line. The vexatious little lump was, also, successfully removed and, touch wood, fingers crossed, there have been no further arguments from her body. Perhaps it has finally given in and accepted its fate. Good riddance!

After these procedures, she was back at home recovering the same day, lump free and that was how we wanted it to remain: no more little surprises, no more warnings and no more breast tissue, ever!

24

Into the Future

"Twenty-five years and my life is still
Trying to get up that great big hill of hope
For a destination."

What now and what comes next? Well, for a long time she was having regular annual check-ups, just to make sure everything was going according to plan and there were no more little scares. Ultimately and understandably, she'd had enough and decided to cancel her last hospital appointment back in 2018. She just couldn't face going over old ground.

Since 2008, Juvenile Gigantomastia took its toll on Ellen's mind and body and the big overriding question is why? Why did it happen? Why does it happen and why to our daughter? What was the cause? I don't think it is sufficient to say it's idiopathic, no known cause. Something must have triggered the phenomenal growth in her breast tissue. Hypothetically, there is a possibility that it could have been an adverse response to the Vasopressin tablets, which she took in 2005. If this is true and I had done something by giving her these tablets, how incredibly guilty do I feel? As mothers, I think we subliminally carry maternal blame and whether it was Vasopressin or not I feel responsible.

Could it have been caused by her body's own allergic reaction to oestrogen? Having been with her every step of the way, I am only too aware of how she can react badly to many different and unexpected triggers. I have read some research that suggests that oestrogen, which promotes female characteristics such as the growth of breasts, is a key player in exacerbating the body's allergic reactions. Oestrogen levels are high throughout puberty, so could it have been an allergic reaction? (Dr Summit Shah, blog: role of oestrogen in allergic reactions).

There is also the issue of it being hereditary. If and when she has her own children, will she have to worry about this same problem happening to them? Is my 'unusual' breast tissue anything to do with what happened? Did I pass on dodgy genetic tissue? I do need to point out that this is not a medical book, and I am in no way trying to impart medical advice. These are my thoughts, observations and suggestions relating to my own experience and knowledge gained about this disease.

The difficulty with Juvenile Gigantomastia is that it is a very rare condition and according to Health Line there are only a hundred trusted source cases that have been reported in the medical literature. The National Library of Medicine (NLM), which is the world's largest biomedical library produces trusted health information and PubMed, is part of this literature and has been available online since 1996 and is maintained by the NLM.

I do wholeheartedly agree with this article written in PubMed:

"...the development of macromastia, or Juvenile Gigantomastia, in adolescence leads to a deforming and distressing condition during a sensitive period in a girl's life. Vulnerability to developing a negative body image and the desire to fit in predisposes these female adolescents to significant psychological stressors. Social issues arise secondary to poor fitting clothing, trouble exercising and public scrutiny resulting from their large breasts. In addition, physical ailments including back pain, shoulder pain and intertrigo (inflammation caused by the rubbing of one area of skin on another), at the inflammatory fold, cause further anguish."

Ellen and what she went through has had the trajectory of her life, her character and her life path changed for good.

Thankfully, there is far more information about the subject now than there was when this all started with my daughter. Any information relating to Juvenile Gigantomastia is so much better than none at all.

One grievance I have is that when reading about the various cases in nearly all of the available literature there is a tendency to group all the females affected and call them women. No, some of these females affected, as in Ellen's case, are not women but prepubescent girls. The definition of a woman is an adult female human being, and the definition of an adult is a person who is fully grown or developed. Neither of these applied to my daughter. I believe that using the term women undermines the terrible social, psychological, and physical aspects of this debilitating and devastating disease.

I don't know whether my daughter's case has been documented or is included somewhere in the annals of medical science. However, at the risk of repeating myself, as a result of the rarity of her condition, the research into this disease is spartan or non-existent. There are too few known cases but that doesn't mean to say that somewhere in the world there isn't a young girl suffering from breasts that are simply too big, with a disease that left unchecked will ultimately ruin her life.

The other question is how big is too big? How big do they have to be before the medical world takes notice? How big would she have grown without these operations?

I believe that her breast size would be too terrible to contemplate, and her life would be impossible; not to put a too finer point on it, her life would be miserable and probably not worth living.

The embarrassment and awkwardness of this condition and the stigma attached are other factors that, perhaps, prevent more girls from coming forward and therefore more research being carried out to find out why? There is and always has been real difficulty in having an open discussion about my daughter's very large breasts. The subject is emotive and in some cases a cause of embarrassment.

The only true facts we do know is that it is a random, hard-hitting, insidious disease, which left to its own devices can cause untold misery and the only solution is at best a reduction or at worst a mastectomy.

The effects of this condition, on Ellen, still continue and there are areas that she would like improved:

- That old problem of the tennis ball which created a big dip in her left armpit is still a dip and an unsightly one at that.
- Her nipples and areola need to be tattooed again and they are asymmetrical.
- She isn't happy with the appearance of her breasts and feels they look fake. They're too firm and full and have no give. She is a little self-conscious of them looking like false breasts and feels that people will assume she had breast augmentation for cosmetic reasons only.
- She does not have a cleavage.
- At some stage, her implants, we know, will have to be replaced.

It was for these reasons, in March 2022, she decided, because she can, to make an appointment with Mr Charmingly-Direct, to find out whether there are any cosmetic procedures that would enhance her look. As well as discussing the need to replace the implants. This was her choice, and it didn't involve me.

I was nervous when I initially booked this appointment but here I was sitting in front of the man who had literally carved up my chest and I felt good! I had no concerning issues or reservations; nothing I was going to discuss was pressing nor was it fundamental to my health mentally or physically. It felt soo nice and I was blessed. I could go ahead with any procedure, or I could not – choice was a lovely thing.

I am very mindful of how far I've come.

"Really good to see you, after all this time." He leapt up from behind his desk and gave me a big hug. He was, as I remember him to be, his charming self. He asked about my life, hobbies, boyfriend, work and family. It was so nice to have this conversation with him, considering ten years and many

operations had passed since we had seen one another.

He recapped on what had happened, reaffirming that it was so very rare, and that the volume of breast tissue was so large and the biggest he or for that matter anybody else had encountered, which meant there was no blueprint that could be followed. My small frame making everything so much more difficult. Apparently, I, or at least my breasts, were the object of a nationwide discussion, oh joy!

"But that's in the past; what can I do to help you now?" I explained that I wanted some cosmetic tweaks, under my armpit, have the implants replaced to encourage more of a drop and provide a more natural look to the breast as well.

Reminiscent of times gone by, I whipped my top off, he examined me and took some images. As always, he was straight to the point and in his professional way explained that my skin was still very fragile. The scarring was much lower on my chest than would normally be expected, due to the huge size and the amount of tissue that was removed. This would make it difficult to hide the scars, although these weren't my main concern because it was the overall shape of my breasts that I wanted improving. My nipples and areola would need further tattooing as well, to enhance the colour.

However, he said "I will give it some thought and see what I can do and contact you outlining the best way forward."

That, for the time being, was all I wanted.

There are other issues, unfortunately, that are unable to be fixed cosmetically, the issue of breastfeeding if and when she becomes a mum. All mothers-to-be are told of the importance of breastfeeding; the advantages far outweigh the disadvantages. "Breast is best," we are told, with breastmilk being the perfect mix of essential nutrients and antibodies. When I had my own three children, I was adamant that this is what I would do and once I had overcome the pain and discomfort of this task, I found it relatively easy. Even though getting to this point wasn't without its difficulties; having to use a selection of lotions and potions on my nipples, smelling of milk when my breasts leaked and mastering the art of feeding a baby who refuses to keep still, leaving you at times very much on display.

Breastmilk offers protection from certain infections and helps to contribute to the baby's long-term health. We are told that breastfed children perform better on intelligence tests, are less likely to be overweight or obese and therefore less prone to diabetes in later life. If this isn't enough to frighten a mother into submission, I don't know what is. But what about those mothers who simply can't produce enough milk, can't feed because of illness or, as in my daughter's case, won't have any milk ducts because the whole kit and caboodle have been taken away?

In June 2018 the Royal College of Midwives published new guidance for mothers, saying the decision to breastfeed – or not – is "a woman's choice and must be respected." Jan Berger, an international board lactation consultant said that good parenting is more important than breastfeeding. These are both very encouraging and surely must help to alleviate the guilt and the feeling of failure that some mothers who can't breastfeed may feel.

I wondered what alternatives my daughter would have when she became a mother. It was heartening to discover that as well as formula, there are donated breastmilk banks if you are determined your baby should have breastmilk. The United Kingdom Association for Milk Banking (UKAMB) makes it possible to order pasteurised human donor milk. All registered donors must undergo lifestyle checks and screening tests and all milk is tested for bacteria and pasteurised for added protection.

The other possibility is wet nursing, which is the act of breastfeeding someone else's child. A wet nurse may have a breast milk supply from feeding her own child, or she may stimulate a supply of breast milk specifically for another woman's child.

I appreciate this might not be everyone's cup of tea, but I am full of admiration for any woman who has done this. With considerable dedication and preparation, breastfeeding without pregnancy (induced lactation) is possible. It involves tricking your body with cues that tell it to produce milk. Induced lactation depends on the successful replication of the hormones, oestrogen, progesterone and human placental lactogen. This hormone therapy may last for months and to increase the supply, pumping must occur on a daily basis. This is a bit forward-thinking on my part, but it would be reassuring to know that if and when my daughter becomes a mother, there are possible options available.

Life, however, I am very pleased to say, has improved considerably and it is essential to look at how far she has come and what has been achieved. If nothing else she has realised that it is so important for her to be able to love her new breasts and not look upon them as the enemy; they are a far cry from that which she suffered before. It is essential for her to continue to feel comfortable and happy with her body and to look at herself with confidence and in the knowledge that she is so much better off than she was all those years ago.

At this particular moment, she is the happiest she has been in a long time. She recognises that her body no longer has a deformity and is grateful for and acknowledges that fact. She is luckier than some people who have permanent disfigurements that can't be fixed with an operation. One thing we have learnt from all this is that life can sometimes be precarious and, when it's going well, it is important to recognise and enjoy it.

I am able to laugh at myself and not take life too seriously, how can I, with a medical history like mine? This ability to laugh at situations, however detrimental, has provided me with comfort and a sense of humour, which is key to so many things.

Whether it is the result of all that has gone on before or whether it was always going to be how I am, I have an innate and intuitive ability to recognise situations or circumstances that will or won't be good for me, and in a way parent myself. It's sometimes hard to explain but going through so much physical and emotional trauma, has resulted in a much more sensitive and limited tolerance for things. I would say I'm hyper-empathetic, possibly as a result of all my operations, which have their pros and cons.

I look after my health probably more so than most at my age and nurture my inner child and all my temperaments, as I know that I am a lot more sensitive to things – both emotionally and physically susceptible. I wouldn't be surprised if I had a strain of PTSD from all of the procedures that took place, which I just had to accept, as choice didn't really come into it.

However, life is short and sweet and testing at times, and I'm glad you've written this book, Mum, as it's easy to forget what happened – I definitely could only recall half of this! I think it's been cathartic and necessary for us both, unknowingly, providing a moment in the business of life to appreciate the trauma and distress that went down – and also revisiting the photos – which shocked me too!

So here we are, fourteen years on from when the whole tragedy began. If we had all known what her fate was going to be would we have been able to deal with it any better? I don't think so and if we could have looked into the future and seen what was going to happen, it wouldn't have been a pretty sight. I think it's best to leave the future to itself and let it unfold as it will but all the while keeping the faith and remaining positive.

As for all her old bras, which are a big part of her story, it is probably time to get rid of them, as they only serve as a reminder of those very distressing times, which thankfully are no more. We won't burn those bras because there are many bra donation services, such as 'Support the Girls', 'Free the Girls', 'The Bra Recyclers', and 'Donate your Bra', to name just a few. We'll happily donate them and hope they provide support and confidence to another girl or woman in need.

You may also remember, way back when, in November 2007, there was an issue with the wing mirror on our car. Well, as this story has proved, some things are quite unbelievable and believe it or not we still drive around in the same car and the funny thing is that we never did get the wing mirror fixed. It is still taped up with electrical tape, used for its durable properties and stretching ability! The tape has been replaced several times over since then.

Perhaps, now, it's also time to make another donation and send the car to the scrapyard and buy ourselves a new one.

As is the case with every story there is no perfect end but just a continuation of an ongoing theme where improvements may lead to some kind of perfection. She dealt with the issues in this story with fortitude, courage, stoicism and acceptance; I do believe she deserves a medal, especially now that she has a near-perfect chest to pin it on. Let's not forget, though, that there isn't a chest out there that is perfect.

This is our daughter's and sister's story and hers alone and we thank you for taking the time to read it. Don't forget that if, at any time, you hear our anthem, crank up the music, sing along, feel its energy, be uplifted and think of how good life can be! And as she says:

When life gives you lemons – squeeze the hell out of them - nobody said life would be easy.

25

Farewell

February 18th 2009 – November 7th 2022

Just as this story was going to print, very, very sadly our beloved dog passed away:

Oh, precious little one
Please, please don't go.
Our love for you is still so new,
Hold on, keep breathing, fight on through.

Oh, my precious little one,
From far away you came to us.
Not wanting, needing any fuss,
Casting your spell so we could be free.

Oh, our precious little one,
Don't struggle with the mortal pain you feel.
Our torment and our grieving,
Is currency for you leaving.

Be gone oh precious little one,
Take flight and rise above.
Take all our love,
Farewell and thanks forever more.

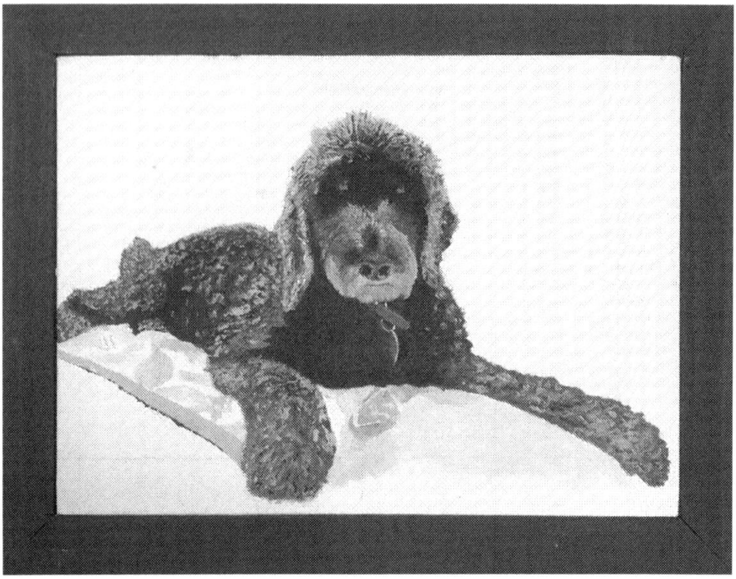

Lyrics

'What's Up?' *by 4 Non Blondes*

Twenty-five years and my life is still
Trying to get up that great big hill of hope
For a destination

I realized quickly when I knew I should
That the world was made up of this brotherhood of man
For whatever that means

And so I cry sometimes
When I'm lying in bed just to get it all out
What's in my head

And I, I am feeling a little peculiar

And so I wake in the morning

And I step outside
And I take a deep breath and I get real high
And I scream from the top of my lungs
"What's going on?"

And I say, "Hey-ey-ey-ey"
Hey-ey-ey
I said, "Hey, what's going on?"

And I say, hey yeah yeah, hey yeah yeah
I said, "Hey, what's going on?"

Oh, oh ooh, ooh, uh-huh
Oh, oh ooh, ooh, uh-huh

And I try, oh my God do I try
I try all the time, in this institution

And I pray, oh my God do I pray
I pray every single day
For a revolution

And so I cry sometimes

When I'm lying in bed
Just to get it all out
What's in my head
And I, I am feeling a little peculiar

And so I wake in the morning
And I step outside
And I take a deep breath and I get real high
And I scream from the top of my lungs
"What's going on?"

And I say, "Hey-ey-ey-ey"
Hey-ey-ey
I said, "Hey, what's going on?"

Twenty-five years and my life is still
Trying to get up that great big hill of hope
For a destination

Acknowledgements

It goes without saying that I wouldn't have written this memoir if it wasn't for Ellen and all that she went through. A heartfelt and bittersweet thanks, with all my love to you.

My Mum who has sat and listened to me throughout, who read the very first draft and thought it was great. Thanks Mum. My mother in-law who would spend time listening and being with Ellen and who sadly passed away before this book became a reality.

Shaun and the boys, I know how much you all struggled and how much you cared, thank you for being you.

To my sister who looked after her when I was working and the rest of the family for being there.

To all my very good friends, you know who you are. You were there at the beginning and shared my concerns, listened to my rantings, and eased what was to be a very difficult path to tread. To Kate Barnham, friend and midwife who was there at her birth, read the second draft, and worried with us and supported me and Ellen through it all. To Louise Clover, author, producer and writer, who read the third script, and whose advice was invaluable. To Jenny Ross, who read I'm not sure which draft it was and who, very thoughtfully, put me in touch with Lisa Mitchell, a freelance Editor whose thoughts and ideas were of tremendous help, putting me firmly in the right direction.

To Keith Abbott and Karolina Robinson from Michael Terence Publishing, a great big thank you for all your support, guidance and expertise, this book would not have happened without you all.

Finally, I cannot end without acknowledging all the medical staff; doctors, nurses, particularly the nurses on the Peanut Ward, and consultants, from all the various hospitals, that helped and supported her.

A great big thank you!

A Note from the Author

In writing this memoir, my intention and probably the most I can expect, is to bring awareness to the condition; Juvenile Gigantomastia, or just Gigantomastia, Macromastia or another name for the same illness, breast Hypertrophy.

If, as a result, what follows is medical research into the cause of this disease, then so much the better.

Prevention, however, is better than cure and to be able to avoid this happening at all, would be my ultimate goal.

Nichola H Walker

Available worldwide from Amazon

Michael Terence Publishing

www.mtp.agency

www.facebook.com/mtp.agency

@mtp_agency

Printed in Great Britain
by Amazon

17342014R10111